EDITH STEIN

OUTSTANDING CHRISTIAN THINKERS

Series Editor: Brian Davies OP, Professor of Philosophy at Fordham University, New York.

The Cappadocians
Anthony Meredith SJ

Hans Urs von Balthasar
John O'Donnell SJ

Augustine
Mary T. Clark RSCJ

Teresa of Avila
Archbishop Rowan Williams

Catherine of Siena
Giuliana Cavallini OP

Bultmann
David Fergusson

Kierkegaard
Julia Watkin

Karl Barth
John Webster

Lonergan
Frederick Crowe SJ

Aquinas
Brian Davies OP

Reinhold Niebuhr
Kenneth Durkin

Paul Tillich
John Heywood Thomas

The Venerable Bede
Benedicta Ward SLG

Karl Rahner
William V. Dych SJ

The Apostolic Fathers
Simon Tugwell OP

Anselm
G. R. Evans

Denys the Areopagite
Andrew Louth

Newman
Avery Cardinal Dulles SJ

Calvin
T. H. L. Parker

Edith Stein
Sarah Borden

EDITH STEIN

Sarah Borden

continuum
LONDON • NEW YORK

Continuum
The Tower Building
11 York Road
London SE1 7NX

15 East 26th Street
New York
NY 10010

www.continuumbooks.com

First published 2003

British Library Cataloguing-in-Publication Data
A catalogue record for this book is available from the British Library.

ISBN 0–8264–5261–2 (Hardback)
     0–8264–5262–0 (Paperback)

Typeset by Fakenham Photosetting Ltd, Fakenham, Norfolk, NR21 8NN
Printed and bound by Biddles Ltd, Guildford and King's Lynn

Contents

Editorial Foreword

St Anselm of Canterbury (1033–1109) once described himself as someone with faith seeking understanding. In words addressed to God he says 'I long to understand in some degree thy truth, which my heart believes and loves. For I do not seek to understand that I may believe, but believe in order to understand.'

This is what Christians have always inevitably said, either explicitly or implicitly. Christianity rests on faith, but it also has content. It teaches and proclaims a distinctive and challenging view of reality. It naturally encourages reflection. It is something to think about; something about which one might even have second thoughts.

But what have the greatest Christian thinkers said? And is it worth saying? Does it engage with modern problems? Does it provide us with a vision to live by? Does it make sense? Can it be preached? Is it believable?

The Outstanding Christian Thinkers series is offered to readers with questions like these in mind. It aims to provide clear, authoritative and critical accounts of outstanding Christian writers from New Testament times to the present. It ranges across the full spectrum of Christian thought to include Catholic and Protestant thinkers, thinkers from East and West, thinkers ancient, mediaeval and modern.

The series draws on the best scholarship currently available, so it will interest all with a professional concern for the history of Christian ideas. But contributors also write for general readers who have little or no previous knowledge of the subjects to be dealt with. Its volumes should therefore prove helpful at a popular as well as an academic level. For the most part they are devoted to a single thinker, but occasionally the subject is a movement or school of thought.

Brian Davies OP

Preface

Edith Stein has been quite famous on the European continent for many years – there have been two commemorative stamps in her honor, and in 1999 she was named co-patroness of Europe, with St Bridget of Sweden and St Catherine of Siena. She has received less attention in the English-speaking world, despite James Collins's 1942 article presenting her as a philosophical force to be reckoned with. This inattention is, I am convinced, a mistake. Stein provides an example of a Christian thinker deeply engaged in the debates of her own day, and her work offers models and insights for addressing the questions of the twenty-first century. I offer this book as a brief introduction and overview of Stein's life and thought.

With the exception of her dissertation, none of Stein's works were written in a university setting, and a number of her most significant books were not published during her lifetime. Perhaps as a result of this, her writings are more often responses to the concerns and needs around her than sustained critiques on a particular topic – it might be appropriate to call her a 'philosopher of the trenches.' Her theory of woman was developed in lectures addressed both to Catholic associations and university audiences in Europe in the midst of the women's movement of the 1920s and 1930s; her analysis of the state was written in postwar Germany amid debates on the proper governance of the defeated state; and her spiritual writings were written for the religious sisters with whom she lived, celebrating special occasions and filling in gaps in their education. An exception to this generalization might be her metaphysical writings, analyses amounting to approximately a thousand pages. These works, written in a mere seven years, however, can also be seen as a response. They are an attempt to come to grips with the theoretical positions encountered with her adoption of Catholicism, to make classical doctrines speak a more modern language, and to weigh the relative merits of two different philosophical traditions, both of which played a significant role in her intellectual formation.

The following chapters are arranged (roughly) chronologically, beginning – after a brief chapter on her life – with her pre-conversion writings and working to her spiritual texts, written during her final decade in the Carmelite order. Stein always wrote in conversation, and I have tried to present the context of her writings as clearly as I am able. That has necessitated relatively detailed discussions of contemporary philosophical schools and medieval metaphysical debates. These debates are, however, not merely 'academic.' For Stein, all intellectual thinking is tied to and grows out of our fundamental concerns and our deepest loves. (For those who simply want a small taste of Stein's thought and would like to avoid the more detailed discussions, I recommend reading the opening chapter and then skipping to Chapters 4, 5, 7, and 8.)

When quoting from Stein's texts, I have used the published English translations available at the time of writing. All quotations from texts not yet published (summer 2002) in translation are my own. A book is always the work of many hands and minds, and I am especially grateful to the Wheaton College Philosophy Department for release time from teaching and to many friends and colleagues who offered comments and suggestions, especially Sr Josephine Koeppel, Mary Wilson, Mindy Zehner, and David Cook.

Sarah Borden
September, 2002

Acknowledgements

There is a large body of scholarship on various aspects of Stein's life and writings, and I have listed a number of important works in the bibliography. Many of my decisions regarding which elements to emphasize, as well as my interpretations, have benefited from this community of scholars. In particular, Marianne Sawicki's lucid analyses (especially in *Body, Text and Science* and her Introduction to *Philosophy of Psychology and the Humanities*) have opened up Stein's early phenomenology, and my presentations in Chapters 2 and 3 – both in general approach and in many details – owe much to her work. Sawicki's interpretations of the early Stein are now, and will surely be for years to come, the benchmark by which Stein scholarship is measured. I am grateful as well for Professor Gerhard Rempel's online lectures on the history of Germany; his clear and orderly history aided me greatly in my research into the cultural and social conditions of Germany during Stein's life. Finally, I would like to mention the research of Sr Josephine Koeppel, Sr Waltraud Herbstrith, and Suzanne Batzdorff on Stein's life. Their careful work has been the basis for many biographies and biographical sketches of Stein, and this book is no exception.

Abbreviations

For full publication details of these works see Select Bibliography, first section: Works by Edith Stein.

CWES   *Collected Works of Edith Stein*
EeS   *Endliches und ewiges Sein* [*ESW* II]
ESW   *Edith Steins Werke*
ESGA   *Edith Stein Gesamtausgabe*
EW   *Essays on Women* [*CWES* 2]
HL   *The Hidden Life: Essays, Meditations, Spiritual Texts* [*CWES* 4]
HT   'Husserl's Phenomenology and the Philosophy of St Thomas Aquinas' (I will be following Baseheart's translation but will provide the page numbers from both English versions.)
KF   *Knowledge and Faith* [*CWES* 8]
Letters *Self-Portrait in Letters 1916–1942* [*CWES* 5] (Note that nos denote letters nos.)
Life   *Life in a Jewish Family* [*CWES* 1]
PE   *On the Problem of Empathy* [*CWES* 3]
PPH   *Philosophy of Psychology and the Humanities* [*CWES* 7]
PPHi   'Sentient Causality' (this is the first essay in the volume above)
PPHii   'Individual and Community' (this is the second essay in the volume above)
SC   *The Science of the Cross* [*ESW* I]
UüS   'Eine Untersuchung über den Staat' (see Bibliography section 'Other Writings'.)
WG   'Ways to Know God', in *Knowledge and Faith* [*CWES* 8]

1

Life and Writings

Edith Stein (1891–1942), who took the religious name Teresa Benedicta à Cruce (Teresa Benedicta of the Cross), was beatified in 1987 and canonized eleven years later on October 11, 1998, by Pope John Paul II.[1] When the beatification process began in 1962, the advocates focused on her life and good works, arguing for her case based on heroic virtue; however, in 1983, Joseph Cardinal Höffner proposed a different route to beatification and sent a letter to Rome requesting that she be considered a martyr because of her clear theology of suffering, her willingness to follow the path of the Cross and offer her life as a sacrifice, and the circumstances under which she, her sister Rosa, and approximately 300 other baptized Christians of Jewish descent were sent to Auschwitz. In 1987 Stein was confirmed by the Congregation for the Causes of Saints both as a martyr and as someone of heroic virtue, the first person confirmed as both in the 400-year history of the Congregation.[2]

Edith Stein grew up in the southeastern region of Germany, Silesia, which was ceded to Poland at the end of the Second World War. Stein's hometown, Breslau (renamed Wroclaw), was the capital of the Silesian area and around 1900 had a population of approximately 400,000. Its size and location made it an important economic and cultural city, boasting the prestigious Friedrich Wilhelm University. The Stein family had moved to Breslau just a few years before Edith's birth, looking for better conditions for their lumber business. But in 1893, when Edith was not yet two, her father died unexpectedly. He had been out inspecting a forest and was overcome by sunstroke. After the death of her husband, Auguste

Stein (against the advice of relatives) took over the lumber company and turned it into a successful business, while Else, the oldest daughter, looked after the children.

Edith was the youngest of the seven children who survived infancy, and her mother attached special importance to the fact that her last child was born on Yom Kippur, the Day of Atonement (October 12, 1891), the holiest day in the Jewish calendar. Her mother was clearly one of Edith's heroes, and throughout her life Auguste Stein, a devout Jew, encouraged her children to attend synagogue and celebrate the Jewish holidays. It is likely, however, that the children received only minimal training in Judaism and learned no Hebrew.

Edith was an extremely bright child, strongwilled, and prone to temper tantrums. The story is told that, when she was five years old, she did not want to go to kindergarten but to first grade with her older sister. She cried and fought daily until Else agreed to speak with the principal. After some persuasion, the principal allowed Edith to skip the second half of kindergarten and join the first-grade class. Edith's attitude changed, however, when, at the age of seven, 'reason assumed command' of her (*Life in a Jewish Family* [hereafter *Life*], p. 75). She began to be docile and obedient, following more readily the advice of others. She says of this transformation: 'I do not know how that happened; I do believe what cured me was the distaste and shame I experienced at the angry outbursts of others and the acute realization I had that the price of such self-indulgence was the loss of one's dignity' (*Life*, p. 75).

As she grew older, she was known as a kind, warm-hearted woman with an unusual ability to empathize with others. As a young girl, however, she gained a reputation for speaking her mind and not being hesitant to criticize others,[3] and she describes her younger self as quite proud of her accomplishments (*Life*, pp. 195–6). Nonetheless, when one of her aunts called her a '*Streberin*,' a go-getter, Edith resented the comment; though proud, she recognized that it was better to be good than clever.

Edith and her sister Erna, who was twenty months older than Edith, were the only Stein children to go to the university; the family valued education, but had not been financially stable enough to pay for the additional schooling when the older children had finished high school. In 1910, Edith enrolled in the Friedrich Wilhelm University with interests in German studies, history, and psychology. Women were first admitted to universities in Germany in 1908, and Edith and Erna were among the first women entering the university in Breslau. During high school, Edith had been active in the women's suffrage movement, and, in college, she joined the Pedagogical Society for Women's Right to Vote and the Women's Student Union. Reflecting back on her college years, Stein describes her younger self as 'a radical feminist' (*Self-Portrait in Letters* [*Letters*], no. 100), and she recounts arguments she and her circle of female friends had regarding how to juggle career and family. Edith Stein was the only one among them to argue consistently that she would not give up her career for the sake of marriage. She notes ironically, however, that she was the only one among the circle who gave up her career upon marriage (her marriage to the Church) (*Life*, p. 123).

During her second year at university, Stein came across references to Edmund Husserl's *Logical Investigations*, one of the most significant philosophical texts published at the turn of the century, and soon decided to spend a semester studying phenomenology with Husserl in Göttingen.[4] She was interested in the claim that Husserl's new philosophical method, phenomenology, could provide a theoretical grounding for the sciences – something Stein thought psychology needed. She describes the psychology she was taught in the early 1900s as studying the person from the outside. She says:

> [a]ll my study of psychology had persuaded me that this science was still in its infancy; it still lacked clear basic concepts; furthermore, there was no one who could establish such an essential foundation. On the other hand, what I had learned about phenomenology, so far, fascinated me tremendously because it consisted precisely of such a labor of clarification, and because, here, one forged one's own mental tools for the task at hand. (*Life*, p. 222)

Thus, Edith and a friend, Rose Guttmann, decided to spend the summer semester pursuing phenomenology.

Göttingen at that time was both the philosophical and spiritual center for phenomenology, which, although gaining attention, was in its infancy. Husserl had worked as a *privatdocent*[5] in Halle for fourteen years and moved to Göttingen in 1901 as *extraordinarius*, the equivalent of an assistant professor. He was viewed as something of an outsider in Göttingen, and the more conservative faculty were a bit suspicious of his new philosophical method. After the publication of *Logical Investigations* in 1900 and 1901, however, Husserl began attracting a following. Numerous students, who have since

3

made a name in their own right, came to Göttingen to study phenomenology with him, among them, Adolf Reinach (1883–1917),[6] Theodor Conrad (1881–1969) and Hedwig Conrad-Martius (1888–1966),[7] Dietrich von Hildebrand (1889–1977),[8] Alexander Koyré (1892–1964),[9] Jean Héring (1890–1966),[10] and Roman Ingarden (1893–1970).[11] In addition to the influence of Husserl, Max Scheler was a strong presence among this group of students; he had moved to Göttingen at the invitation of Dietrich von Hildebrand after losing his post at the University of Munich and lectured in local coffee shops, primarily on the phenomenology of religion and ethics.[12]

Stein arrived in 1913, the year Husserl's *Ideas I* was published in the phenomenological journal *Jahrbuch für Philosophie und phänomenologische Forschung*,[13] and quickly joined the Philosophical Society, led by Adolf Reinach, Husserl's current *privatdocent*. Reinach became one of Stein's close friends and introduced her both to Husserl and to Husserl's thought. The Master, as Husserl was affectionately called, was unfortunately not known for being a clear lecturer, although universally recognized as brilliant and much beloved; thus, it was Reinach's task to clarify the phenomenological project for the newcomers. By the end of the summer semester, Stein decided not to return to Breslau, as she had originally planned, but instead to pursue phenomenology in Göttingen with Reinach, Husserl, and with the Philosophical Society.

The years at Göttingen were important ones, and Stein nostalgically recalls the delight and charm of the pre-war Göttingen (*Life*, p. 239). She was twenty-one when she arrived, full of expectation and deeply attracted to the new philosophy. The year 1914, however, changed Göttingen and the circle she had joined. With the advent of the First World War, Stein's close friend Roman Ingarden returned to his native Poland, and the group's leader, Adolf Reinach, volunteered for service. (Reinach would not have been drafted, but he chose to go and was killed at the front in Belgium in 1917.) One of Husserl's sons was killed in Flanders, and other members of the Philosophical Society joined the armed services. Edith returned to Breslau, began medical training at All Saints Hospital, and signed on with the Red Cross for unconditional service to be sent wherever there was need. In October of 1914 she returned to Göttingen, still awaiting the call to service. During this time, she completed her exams (with highest honors) and began research for her dissertation. Early in 1915 the call from the Red Cross came, and Stein, against her mother's wishes, accepted an assignment at a hospital for contagious diseases in Mährisch-Weisskirchen, Austria. She worked there for six months and received a medal of valor for her courage and service at the hospital.

After serving with the Red Cross and teaching briefly in Breslau, Stein returned to her philosophical studies, following Husserl to Freiburg, where he had been offered a full professorship. For her dissertation, Stein chose to write on the problem of empathy, or how we have access to another's experience. Throughout his work, Husserl struggled with the specter of solipsism; phenomenology requires one to bracket all presuppositions, including claims about existence. In so doing, one can study what we actually experience, without the distraction of many judgments we habitually overlay on our experiences. Phenomenology runs the risk, however, of appearing to be trapped in one's own head. If claims regarding the existence of objects are bracketed, what status does another's experience have? Stein recognized that dealing with the threat of solipsism is necessary if one is to make phenomenology a respectable and desirable method, and thus she focused on how we have insight into what another person experiences.

Stein went through several dark periods as she wrote her dissertation. At one point, she says that she would not have cared if a car ran her over in the street or if she fell off a cliff (*Life*, p. 278). Reinach offered her encouragement at critical moments, and Husserl seemed quite pleased with the final product. Stein received her PhD *summa cum laude* in 1916. During the eighteen months following the completion of her PhD, Stein worked for Husserl. She was not hired as *privatdocent*, as Adolf Reinach had been, but rather worked as his private assistant. This position lacked affiliation with the university, although it appears that the work was similar: Edith taught 'phenomenological kindergarten,' as she called it, prepared students to take Husserl's courses, and edited manuscripts, preparing them for publication.[14] (Husserl would not review many of the manuscripts; he would lose interest in previous writings and move on to something new.) During Edith's work with Husserl, few of the major writings she edited and prepared made it to press.

Letters to various friends reveal a great deal of frustration with the working relationship with Husserl. She clearly respected him, but found his failure to review her work or to collaborate with her, sources of irritation. In 1918 she quit in order to focus on her own work, and moved back to Breslau, living with her mother and twelve or so relatives. The shortage of housing after the war made such living arrangements common in Germany. Edith continued tutoring students in phenomenology and wrote three major treatises in phenomenology, all of which were published in Husserl's *Jahrbuch*.

There have been a surprising number of students in the phenomenological movement, particularly among those studying with Husserl, who have come to the Christian faith. After having consciously given up prayer at the age of fifteen, Edith was among those who found themselves drawn back to God while studying at Göttingen. The phenomenological method itself is not explicitly Christian, but it does require an open consideration of all phenomena. One of the requirements of phenomenology is that we bracket our presuppositions and study our experiences (including religious ones) prior to making judgments about them. Therefore, any prejudices against religion would have to be bracketed in order to engage adequately in the phenomenological method. Stein was also in contact with Scheler, who was outspoken about religious issues and applied the phenomenological method to phenomena of faith; Stein's close friend Hedwig Conrad-Martius was a devout Lutheran; and Husserl himself had been baptized as a Lutheran in Vienna when he was in his twenties. Thus, it is not surprising that religious concerns were in the forefront of her thoughts.

There were also more personal experiences that were important for Stein's conversion. After the death of her husband, Anna Reinach and Edith worked together on Adolf Reinach's papers, and Stein saw in Anna a model of courage and peace in the face of tragedy. Stein says that, while she had initially thought that she was there to offer comfort to Anna, it was Anna who offered her Christ's strength in the face of an unbearable tragedy.

While in Breslau, after working for Husserl, Stein regularly attended both the synagogue with her mother and mass at a local parish, and by 1920 Stein was trying to decide if she would enter the Evangelical Lutheran Church or the Roman Catholic Church. In 1921, while visiting Hedwig Conrad-Martius in Bergzabern, Edith picked up St Teresa of Avila's autobiography. She stayed up all night to finish it, and when morning came, she said, 'this is the truth.' The next day she bought a catechism and missal and, soon after, went to the local parish and asked to be baptized. The priest told her that it was customary to take a class preparing one for baptism; she told him to test her, and he found she could answer all the catechism questions. She was baptized on January 1, 1922.

There are various stories regarding why Stein converted to Christianity. Most frequently, her reading of Teresa of Avila's autobiography is cited as the main reason, and it is likely the proximate cause for her decision to join the Catholic Church (see *Letters*, no. 158a). It appears, however, that other events were also influential. A close friend and intellectual adviser, Erich Przywara (1889–1972), attributes her decision to a personal retreat she once described to him. She had come across a copy of St Ignatius Loyola's *Spiritual Exercises* at a bookshop and decided to do a 30-day 'retreat', although she was a professed atheist at the time. Przywara reports that she came out of the retreat with the decision to convert.[15] In her autobiography, Stein describes another experience that impressed her: while sightseeing at a cathedral, a woman out on her daily shopping trip stopped by the church simply to pray for a few moments, taking a small break to have an intimate conversation with God (*Life*, p. 401). A similar experience occurred on a hiking trip, when Edith and her company stopped to sleep over at a farmhouse. In the morning the farmer and all his workers began the day with prayer. Hedwig Conrad-Martius, while not questioning the sincerity of Stein's conversion, suggests that dashed hopes in a relationship played a role in the timing of her decision. Characteristically, Stein responded to questions about her decision to convert with *Secretum meum mihi* ('My secret belongs to me').

Edith continued living in her mother's house, but her conversion to Catholicism was a source of tension. Each day she would slip out to daily mass, and, while aware of her daughter's absence, Auguste Stein never asked where she went. The tension between Edith and her mother regarding her conversion and especially her decision, eleven years later, to enter a Carmelite monastery, continued for years. Edith had left the religion of the family as anti-Semite feelings were on the rise, and her entrance into the monastic life coincided with increasing, explicit attacks on Jews. (After Stein entered the Carmelite monastery, Auguste refused to write or acknowledge her daughter's weekly letters for the first year. One day in 1935, however, Frau Stein, who was eighty-five at the time, went to visit the building site for a new Carmelite monastery near Breslau. She did not inform her daughters at home that she was going, but shortly thereafter she began adding a small note to the letters sent to Edith [*Life*, Chronology, p. 427].) One afternoon, after Stein had announced her intentions to her family, Edith's twelve-year-old niece asked her why she was entering a convent now. Edith responded that her intention was not to leave her family or the Jewish people. The convent would not keep her immune from the events affecting her people.

In 1923, the year following her baptism and a decade before her acceptance of the veil, Stein moved to Speyer and began teaching at a girls' high school and teachers' training institute of the Dominican nuns of St Magdalena. She had applied for a university post at Göttingen in 1919, and her phenomenological works from this time were intended as the *Habilitationsschrift*, a second doctoral thesis necessary in Germany to obtain a university position. Husserl had written a letter of recommendation that, after great praise, ended with, '[s]hould the academic profession become open to women, I would recommend Dr Stein immediately and most warmly for qualification as a university lecturer.'[16] She did not get the position. Stein then wrote a letter to the Prussian Ministry for Science, Art and Education in protest of the discrimination in academia against women. Approximately a year later, on February 21, 1921, Minister Becker issued a statement declaring that gender should not be used as an obstacle to habilitation. (Although Stein's letter resulted in a public statement from Berlin, 30 years passed before a woman held a post in philosophy in a German university.)[17] Many years earlier an uncle had encouraged both Edith and her sister Erna to enter medical professions; he thought that they would have better chances for advancement as both Jewish and female in the freer field of medicine. Erna followed his advice, but Edith did not, and Erna was able to pursue her career in a way that Edith never could (*Life*, pp. 64–5).

At St Magdalena's in Speyer, Stein taught Latin, Greek and German history. She was a well-liked, although rigorous teacher, and was quite unusual for a girls' school teacher in the 1920s for introducing current political topics, social problems and sex education (see *Letters*, nos 122 and 123). In addition to her teaching duties, Stein was enlisted in several academic projects. She had begun translating Henry Cardinal Newman's *The Idea of a University*, but rather than finishing that, Fr Pryzwara asked her to translate a volume of Newman's diaries and papers. She completed the volume written between 1801 and Newman's conversion to Catholicism.

During this time, the conviction was growing in her that she needed to learn more about the philosophical roots of Catholicism. As a second translation project, Pryzwara encouraged her to turn to Aquinas's *Quaestiones disputatae de veritate* (*Disputed Questions on Truth*). This translation, or as she called it, a paraphrase, was a bit unorthodox; she decided that what was needed was a work which encouraged medieval thought to 'dialogue' with contemporary philosophy and philosophical approaches. Thus, she translated the body of each of the 29 questions, dropping the objections and replies, and included brief commentary as she thought it useful in the text. This work comprises two volumes, and later Stein compiled an index of the German–Latin equivalences used. Many of the terms that she chose have Kantian and phenomenological overtones, and her translation may have made transcendental reading of Thomas Aquinas easier.

Out of these works came three significant original works. The first was an essay comparing the thought of Husserl and St Thomas Aquinas (c. 1225–74). The piece had originally been written as a dialogue between Husserl and Thomas, but Martin Heidegger, who edited the *Festschrift* volume it came out in, did not like the style and asked Stein to rewrite it in a more traditional form.[18] The second was *Potenz und Akt* (*Potency and Act*), which Stein significantly revised between 1935 and 1936 and attempted to publish as *Endliches und ewiges Sein* (*Finite and Eternal Being*). This third work, which Stein calls a 'coming together' of phenomenology and Thomism, is often considered her opus. While Husserl and Thomas Aquinas are the primary influences, one can also see the impact of Hedwig Conrad-Martius, G. W. F. Hegel (1770–1831), John Duns Scotus (c. 1265–1308), and Martin Heidegger. There is an apocryphal story that Heidegger asked Stein for her comments on his text *Being and Time*; Stein came to his office and, without a word, dropped her work on Being and Eternity on his desk. (The original manuscript of *Finite and Eternal Being* appended a long critique of Heidegger, which was dropped from the 1950 version. It has since been published in *Edith Steins Werke* [*ESW*] VI.)

During her eight years teaching at Speyer, Stein took three private vows of poverty, chastity and obedience and committed herself to a regular schedule of prayer and meditation, visiting the Benedictine monastery in Beuron regularly. In 1927 she began lecturing at educational workshops and various meetings in Prague, Vienna, Salzburg, Aachen, Basel, Paris, Münster and Bendorf on women and issues in women's education as well as occasional lectures on several Catholic saints. The lectures were generally very well received, and one audience member at a 1930 lecture in Salzburg enthusiastically wrote:

Edith Stein spoke for almost two hours. For two whole hours, over midday in August, about a thousand people listened to her without making a sound. No scraping of feet, no clearing of throats, no cough could be heard. Captivated, we all listened to that delicate woman who spoke with charming simplicity, her refined face now and then animated by an indefinable smile, in a soft, clear voice, audible to the farthest corners. Not even the tiniest piece of paper did she have before her. Her hands remained quietly folded on the lectern, and yet a restrained dynamic was contained in every sentence. I cannot remember having felt tired for even one minute. For here one sensed a great power of mind, a rich, yet disciplined inner life, born of utmost self-assurance.[19]

In 1932 she began delivering radio addresses on the Bayrische Rundfunk, the Bavarian Radio Network. These lectures and addresses brought her a good deal of publicity, and in 1931 Stein attempted once again to obtain a university post. She inquired into positions at both Freiburg and Breslau, and *Potency and Act* was written as her *Habilitationsschrift*. Once again, Stein's applications were rejected (her reader at Freiburg, Martin Honecker, seems to have been dissatisfied with her integration of Husserlian and Thomistic thought); however, in 1932 she was offered a position at the German Institute for Scientific Pedagogy in Münster. In addition to teaching, she was given the task of preparing a curriculum specifically geared toward teaching women. This project was never completed. Stein lost the position because she was of Jewish descent in April 1933. Ironically, when she lost her position, she had been working with authorities in Berlin on a reform for teaching in the higher grades.

Stein's autobiographical writings emphasize her German heritage and interest in German history and literature. A great motivation for volunteering with the Red Cross was a strong love for her country. Stein reports a comment Reinach made that expressed her own feelings: when asked if he must go to war, he replied, 'It's not that I *must*; rather, I'm permitted to go' (*Life*, p. 294). While these sentiments are most likely true descriptions of her feelings at the beginning of the First World War, they were written down nearly two decades later in a strongly anti-Semitic atmosphere. Stein may have felt a need to emphasize *both* her German-ness and her Jewish-ness. Following the First World War and the 1919 Weimar constitution, there was general optimism among the Jewish community that full equality and admittance into German society was imminent. Jews had been granted citizenship in 1812, but the public had not supported the move, and there had been a strong backlash. In 1869 the North German Confederation had once again granted Jews full citizenship (this extended to the full German Empire in 1871), and while this eliminated the final legal barrier to full social equality, Jews were still rare in the officer corps, public office, and teaching positions. In 1909 only 25 Jews in Germany held the rank of full professor. With the new constitution, it appeared once again as if full equality was in sight. Stein seemed to share this optimism and fervor for an equal society. Events following the First World War, however, indicated that anti-Semitism was still strong. (An early indication of such anti-Semitism was a postwar census evaluating Jewish participation in the war. While the results were never published – most likely because the results did not please the parties ordering the census – the fact that there was such a census raised suspicions and fed anti-Semitic sentiments.)[20]

While it is not fully known how actively involved Stein was in the resistance activities in Germany during this time, clearly the increasing hatred of Jews was a great concern of hers. Her 1925 essay on the state is more critical of racist and totalitarian trends in Germany than most phenomenological essays of that time, and a primary motivation for writing her autobiography in the 1930s was concern about the treatment of Jews in Germany. In 1933 Stein's spiritual adviser encouraged her to write about her life, and in the Introduction, Stein says:

> [w]hat I shall write down on these pages is not meant to be an apologia for Judaism. To develop the 'idea' of Judaism and to defend it against false interpretations ... I would like to give, simply, a straightforward account of my own experience of Jewish life as one testimony to be placed alongside others, already available in print or soon to be published. (*Life*, p. 24)

It appears that she wanted to publish a work that showed how normal and 'German' Jews in Germany truly were, an attempt to demystify the Jewish people. Unfortunately, *Life in a Jewish Family* was not published until 1965.[21]

There were anti-Semite sentiments long before the rise of Hitler, but his election as chancellor on January 30, 1933, made them explicit government policy. Soon after his inauguration, a boycott of Jewish-owned business was begun. In the same year, Stein attempted to get a private audience with Pope Pius XI, but since 1933 was considered a holy year (the 1900th anniversary of Jesus's death) and there were many pilgrimages to Rome, a private audience was not possible, although participation in a group visiting the Pope might have been possible. She then wrote a detailed letter that called for a papal encyclical denouncing the treatment of the Jews in Nazi

Germany and argued that National Socialism was not simply a political party but a worldview that would have repercussions against Christians as well as Jews. She received only a kind letter back, sending blessings to her and her family.[22]

Stein was adamantly and consistently critical of National Socialism. She regularly attended meetings of a student group in Münster protesting against the National Socialists, and after entering the convent, she spoke forcefully about the need to vote against Hitler. Her mother of novices writes:

> ... everyone was frightened by the violence and cruelty of the state authorities. Even in the Cologne Carmel, therefore, there was much uncertainty about how one should behave. Already the Gestapo had arrived at many religious houses without warning and simply turned the religious out, leaving them unprovided for on the street. For a long time the Cologne Carmel had been expecting this same fate, which would almost certainly befall them if they displeased the authorities. Well-meant advice to have nothing to do with the elections was therefore unacceptable. Most of the community adopted the attitude that it did not matter how one voted since the election in any case was being engineered by the Nazis, who would concoct whatever results they pleased.
>
> In the passionate attacks which Sister Benedicta made upon this attitude one could scarcely recognize her for the gentle and retiring person she generally was. Time and again she urged the Sisters not to choose Hitler no matter what the consequences either to individuals or to the community.[23]

This attitude can be seen again in Stein's greeting to the police in Maastricht, the Netherlands, when she was called up before the authorities. Rather than the customary *'Heil Hitler'* or a prudent silence, she opened with *'Gelobt sei Jesus Christus'* ('Praised be Jesus Christ,' a customary greeting in Catholic parts of Germany).

The atmosphere in Germany and the loss of her position at Münster ended Stein's pursuit of an academic life. Ever since her conversion, she had wanted to enter the Carmelite order but had been advised against it because her education and skills could be better used outside the cloister. With that now impossible, however, Stein saw the opportunity to pursue a way of life that she had desired for the past decade. Despite an invitation to teach in South America, Stein chose the contemplative life, and on October 14, 1933, she entered the Carmelite monastery at Lindenthal in Cologne. The clothing ceremony was on April 14, 1934; Hedwig Conrad-Martius came to the ceremony, and many of her friends from her student days, including Husserl, sent greetings and good wishes. She took the name of Teresa Benedicta à Cruce, taking temporary vows on April 21, 1935 and final vows on April 21, 1938.

Stein's intentions upon entering the Carmelite monastery were to give up her scholarly work and join in the life and activities of the community. Except for her superiors, the sisters were unaware of her former life as a scholar, lecturer, and translator, and she was known in the convent as one rather inept at household tasks. There are stories of her finishing sewing projects, which were then quietly slipped to someone else for re-working, and her novice-mistress reports that 'it was positively painful watching her trying to do housework.'[24] Despite her ineptitude in some aspects of monastery life, she reports this time as among the most enjoyable of her life – she says that she laughed more than she had ever before.

After her novitiate, the provincial suggested that she be exempted from some of her household chores and dedicate more time to writing.[25] One of her first projects was reworking *Potency and Act*. Hedwig Conrad-Martius supplied Edith with current literature she requested, which included among other things, Alexander Pfänder's *Die Seele des Menschen* (The Soul of Man), published in 1933, and the most current work on atomic theory. After significant rewriting, she attempted to publish it as *Finite and Eternal Being*. (The Carmelite order paid 3,000 marks to have the manuscript typed, and the press, Borgmeyer, which had published her translation of *De veritate*, set it. Because of the laws preventing non-Aryan publications, however, the press suggested that it be published under another sister's name. Both Stein and the other sister refused. Stein then wrote to friends at the State University of New York, Buffalo, to see if it could be published in the United States; however, it appears that this query did not go very far. The work did not come out until 1950, eight years after Stein's death.) This text was Stein's last work with a distinctively Thomist flavor, and after the failure to get it published, she turned her attention to mystical and theological writings, composed largely for the benefit of the sisters.[26]

While Stein was within the cloister, the Nuremberg Laws were enacted (1935), which defined a Jew as a person whose grandparents were Jewish and which deprived Jews of legal rights. In 1936 the Nazis marched into the Rhineland, and in March 1938 Hitler invaded Austria; by September he had captured the Sudetenland. On the evening of Kristallnacht, 'the Night of Broken Glass' (November

9–10, 1938), the synagogue Stein's mother attended was among the 12,000 synagogues, Jewish homes and businesses destroyed. Because of the increasing violence against Jews, there were fears for the safety of the monastery and sisters in Cologne, and Stein moved to a German Carmelite monastery in Echt, in the southern Netherlands, on New Year's Eve, 1938.[27] Edith's older sister Rosa, who had been baptized after the death of their mother in September 1936, joined Edith in Echt in 1939 as an extern.

In 1940 the Nazis marched into the Netherlands, Belgium and France, and in 1941 the Jews in these countries lost their citizenship. On September 1, 1941, all Jews over the age of six were required to wear a yellow star, and by October 14, the systematic deportation of Jews had begun. In January and March of 1942 both Edith and Rosa were required to appear before the authorities in Maastricht and Amsterdam (*Letters*, no. 337). Concerns about safety arose again, and Stein wrote to friends in Switzerland regarding a possible transfer. The Carmel in Le Pâquier, Switzerland, welcomed Edith, but they were unable to provide space for Rosa. Edith refused to go without her sister, and further inquires were made. Eventually, a convent of active religious was found that could accommodate Rosa, but exit visas from the Netherlands were still needed.

In mid July of 1942, the Catholic bishops sent a telegram to the Reichkommissar, which read:

The undersigned religious organizations of the Netherlands, deeply shaken by the measures against the Jews which have excluded them from the normal life of the people, have learnt with terror of the latest regulations by which men, women, children and whole families are to be deported to the territory of the German Reich. The suffering which has thus been imposed on thousands of people, the awareness that these regulations offend the deepest moral convictions of the Netherlands people, and above all, the denial in these regulations of God's precepts of justice and mercy, force the undersigned religious organizations to request most urgently that these regulations shall not be carried out. On behalf of those Jews who are Christians we wish to emphasize further that these regulations will cut them off from the normal life of the Church.[28]

The Nazi authorities agreed – at least temporarily – to exempt from deportation all Jews who had converted to Christianity prior to January 1, 1941, and on July 24, a warning was sent to the Church leaders, discouraging public protests against Nazi policies. Nonetheless, on Sunday, July 26, the Catholic bishops, along with nine other denominational churches, had a pastoral letter incorporating the telegram read from the pulpits. The next day, the Reichkommissar Seyss-Inquart ordered that all Catholics of Jewish descent be deported by the end of the week. During the next few days, the SS made a sweep of the monasteries in the Netherlands, arresting all non-Aryan members of religious communities. Both Edith and Rosa were arrested on August 2, around five o'clock in the afternoon, and sent to the transit camp in Amersfoort. From there they were shipped to Westerbork, where 1,200 Catholic Jews had been interned.

Reports from people at the camp indicate that Edith and the other members of religious orders continued to pray regularly during the journey; mass was said to the jeers of the SS, and the *Confiteor* was sung daily. Edith was said to have spent the days comforting and assisting the mothers and children. The final report of her life is the testimony of a postal employee on the train platform in Breslau. He says that a woman in a Carmelite habit stood in the doorway of a train as it stopped in Breslau and told him that this was her hometown. The train was heading east. According to Red Cross records, both Edith and Rosa arrived in Auschwitz on August 7 and were gassed in Birkenau on August 9.

For several years, it was still not known for sure whether Edith Stein was alive – there were various rumors placing Edith and Rosa in Teresienstadt, in a Litzmannstadt hospital and in Ravensbrück – and not until the 1958 Red Cross reports was it confirmed that the Stein sisters died in Auschwitz in 1942, within a few days of arriving at the camp. In a beautiful tribute to Edith, Fritz Kaufmann, a close friend from her Göttingen days, wrote:

> I am disconsolate at Edith Stein's death though I am still hoping – perhaps, against hope – that the news will not prove true. With Hans Lipps and her my best Göttingen friends are gone, and life seems so much poorer. It is as if a door to a beloved room of the past had been definitely locked. You can hardly imagine what [Edith Stein] meant to me during the First World War when she did everything to keep me spiritually alive and abreast with the intellectual events within our movement and outside. She was the kind genius of our whole circle, taking care of everything and everybody with truly sisterly love (also of Husserl who was seriously ill in 1918). She was like a guardian angel to Lipps in

the years of his distress. When I spoke to her last time in the Cologne monastery – a lattice between her room and mine – the evening twilight made her fade to my eyes: I felt I was not to see her again. But who could have thought that these beasts would not stop in their cruelty even before a nunnery, and that she would have to die as she may have done? She had joined the Carmelites' order on account of her special veneration for Santa Theresa, but also because she wanted to offer her life and her prayers, in this ascetic community, to save mankind. Did she succeed, after all, in this highest task? (September 9, 1945)[29]

With the opening of the beatification process, numerous letters and testimonies were gathered, many of which cited Stein's intense prayer life, patience and great compassion, and her significance for their own conversions. Her own letters testify to an ongoing ministry of spiritual mentorship, and few who have read her writings can deny that her lifelong search was for truth, her abiding love, for the Cross, and her great hope, that her life may be poured out in love for others.

After Stein's arrest and deportation, many of her papers were gathered and stored by her religious sisters in the Netherlands. During the Germans' retreat on January 6, 1945, however, the sisters were forced to flee the monastery and leave the papers unprotected. A few days after their flight, one sister managed to return and gather the material; unfortunately, amid the destruction and in their cramped quarters, there was nowhere to store them, and the sacks of documents were left lying in the open. In March of 1945, Fr Hermann van Breda (founder of the Husserl Archiv in Leuven), the Carmelite Prior of Geleen, and two sisters went to the ruined convent where the papers had been abandoned, and gathered what was left. The townspeople joined in the task, turning over whatever scraps of paper could be found. The papers were stored at the Husserl Archives until the mid 1950s when Lucy Gelber removed them to her home in order better to protect them. Dr Gelber spent many years organizing the damaged documents and reconstructing Stein's texts, and the publication of the *Edith Steins Werke [ESW]* (Works of Edith Stein) began in 1950 with the first texts assembled.

Notes

1 The Catholic Church follows an extensive process in its recognition and declaration of saints. There are three general stages: the opening of the process (the title *Servant of God* is given); beatification (the title

Blessed is given); and canonization (the person is recognized as a saint). A saint is understood as a person who has 'practiced heroic virtue and lived in fidelity to God's grace' and is put forward by the Church as a model of holiness and as an intercessor (*Catechism of the Catholic Church* (Washington, DC: United States Catholic Conference, Inc.– Liberia Editrice Vaticana, 1994)).

2 Kenneth Woodward gives a short history of Stein's path to beatification in *Making Saints: How the Catholic Church Determines Who Becomes a Saint, Who Doesn't, and Why* (New York: Simon & Schuster, 1990), see esp. pp. 135–44. See also Ambrose Eszer's 'Edith Stein, Jewish Catholic Martyr,' trans. John Sullivan, in John Sullivan (ed.), *Edith Stein Symposium: Teresian Culture* (Carmelite Studies 4) (Washington, DC: ICS Publications, 1987), esp. p. 314.

3 After her conversion, Stein tried to use her ability to find others' weaknesses quickly, as a way to protect rather than to condemn them.

4 Edmund Husserl (1859–1938) is usually considered the founder of *phenomenology*, one of the most influential philosophical movements of the twentieth century.

5 A *privatdocent*, or *Privatdozent*, is a lecturer who, although authorized to teach, is not paid directly by the university.

6 Reinach, who was trained as a legal theorist, is best known for his application of phenomenology to legal theory.

7 Hedwig Conrad-Martius studied psychology under Alexander Pfänder before moving to Göttingen to study with Husserl. Stein was attracted to the Göttingen Philosophical Society in part because of the prominence of the women students there, and Conrad-Martius's philosophical works deeply influenced her own thinking. Both Hedwig and her husband, Theodor Conrad, became close friends of Stein's.

8 Von Hildebrand is perhaps best known for his role in the realist school of phenomenology and his articulate defenses of and writings on the Catholic faith. In 1938 he emigrated to the United States, bringing his developments of phenomenology with him, and taught at Fordham University in New York City.

9 The Russian-born Koyré was a historian of scientific thought, famous for his work on Galileo.

10 Héring helped bring phenomenology to France, although much of his later work was in theology.

11 Roman Ingarden, a native of Poland, is best known for his works on aesthetics, his criticisms of Husserl's transcendental idealism, and his influence on the thought of Pope John Paul II.

12 Scheler (1874–1928) was a contemporary of Husserl's, and like Husserl had a Jewish background but converted to Christianity. (Lutheranism for Husserl, Catholicism for Scheler.)

13 The *Jahrbuch* (in English, the Yearbook for Philosophy and Phenomenological Research) was started by Edmund Husserl, Alexander Pfänder, and Max Scheler in 1913 to be a forum for research in phenomenology. Most of the pieces published in the *Jahrbuch* are book-length studies, not short essays common in most journals. The majority of Husserl's works (at least those which he allowed to be published) were first printed here, as well as several of Stein's pieces.

14 The primary manuscripts Stein worked on were *Ideas II* and *III* and *Lectures on Internal Time-Consciousness*.

15 See 'Die Frage Edith Stein' in Przywara's *In und Gegen: Stellungnahmen zur Zeit* (Nuremberg: Glock & Lutz, 1955).

16 Quoted in Maria Amata Neyer's *Edith Stein: Her Life in Photos and Documents* (Washington, DC: ICS Publications, 1999), p. 30. For the complete letter, see Waltraud Herbstrith (ed.), *Edith Stein: Ein Lebensbild in Zeugnissen und Selbstzeugnissen* (Mainz: Matthias Grünewald, 1998).

17 See Elizabeth Boedeker and Maria Meyer-Plath, *50. Jahre Habilitation von Frauen in Deutschland* (The Hague: Martinus Nijhoff, 1987). See also Koeppel's *Edith Stein: Philosopher and Mystic* (Collegeville, MN: Liturgical Press, 1990), esp. Chapter 8. In a letter to Fritz Kaufmann, Stein says, '[t]he circular to the universities regarding the habilitation of women was due to my request, certainly, but I promise myself very little by way of results' (*Letters*, no. 36).

18 Heidegger (1889–1976), who worked as Husserl's assistant soon after Stein, is among the most significant philosophers of the twentieth century; his most famous work is *Being and Time*.

19 Andrea Loske in Waltraud Herbstrith (ed.), *Never Forget: Christian and Jewish Perspectives on Edith Stein*, trans. Susanne Batzdorff (Washington, DC: ICS Publications, 1998), pp. 239–40.

20 Susanne Batzdorff gives an excellent history of Jews in Germany in *Aunt Edith: The Jewish Heritage of a Catholic Saint* (Springfield, IL: Templegate, 1998), see esp. Chapters 1–3.

21 In Stein's will, dated June 9, 1939, she asks that this work not be published until the death of all her siblings. Perhaps she realized that it could not be published for its original purpose and hoped that she could at least avoid making her family into an unnecessary exhibition. After Erna Biberstein (*née* Stein) reviewed it, an abridged version was published in 1965. An unabridged version did not come out until 1985, several years after Erna's death.

22 Stein's letter may have influenced Pope Pius XI's 1938 decision to have Fr John La Farge and Fr Grundlach draft an encyclical against racism and antisemitism. See Jan H. Nota's 'Edith Stein und der Entwurf für eine Enzyklika gegen Rassismus und Antisemitismus' in *Freiburger Rundbrief, Beiträge zur christlich-jüdischen Begegnung*, 26.97/100 (1974): 35–41.

23 Teresa Posselt, *Edith Stein*, trans. Cecil Hastings and Donald Nicholl (London, New York: Sheed & Ward, 1952), 182–3.

24 Ibid., p. 137. See also Freda Mary Oben, 'Edith Stein the Woman' in *Edith Stein Symposium: Teresian Culture*, p. 25.

25 Waltraud Herbstrith claims that one of Stein's significant contributions to the religious life was the way in which she broke the mold and showed that female contemplatives could do intellectual work (as their male counterparts had been doing for centuries), and not simply needlepoint and embroidery. See Christina Kerstin Oldfelt's 'Aspects of the Religious Experience of Edith Stein as Seen from a Perspective of Analytical Psychology' (diploma thesis, C. G. Jung Institute, Zürich, 1990), p. 2.

26 One notable exception to this is an article Stein wrote in 1941, 'Ways to Know God.'

27 The monastery in Echt was founded in 1875 during the *Kulturkampf* (culture war). Fearing that Catholics would have divided loyalties and thus weaken the recently unified Germany, Bismarck embarked on an ultimately unsuccessful fight to weaken the Catholic Church in Germany, ordering, among other things, the dissolution of all religious communities not involved in the care of the sick. The monastery in Echt where Stein was transferred was originally founded during this period by displaced German religious.

28 Repr. in Posselt *Edith Stein*, p. 203. The pastoral letter including this telegram was not the only letter sent out by the Dutch bishops condemning National Socialism.

29 Quoted in Steven Payne, 'Edith Stein: A Fragmented Life' in *America*, 179.10 (October 10, 1998): 14.

2

Phenomenology and the Person

In 1913 Stein made a decision that would mark her whole intellectual life. She left her widowed mother, her community, and her hometown in order to study in Göttingen with the leader of the most recent philosophical movement. She appears never to have regretted the decision, and all of her philosophical and theological writings are marked by Edmund Husserl's influence. Stein, however, wrote only four strictly phenomenological works: her 1916 dissertation (*On the Problem of Empathy*) and three extended essays published in the preeminent journal for phenomenological research, *Jahrbuch für Philosophie und phänomenologische Forschung*. (Husserl's *Jahrbuch*, as it is commonly referred to, was the central place for presenting phenomenological research and is famous for a number of significant publications, including Husserl's *Ideas I* (1913), Scheler's *Ethics* (1913), and Heidegger's *Being and Time* [1927].) Stein's first two *Jahrbuch* essays, 'Sentient Causality' and 'Individual and Community,' develop themes from her dissertation, and the third, 'Eine Untersuchung über den Staat' (UüS [An Investigation of the State]), puts forward her theory of state structure. A brief introduction to phenomenology will be followed by discussions of Stein's phenomenological work, as developed in her first two publications, focusing on her theories of empathy, causality and motivation, the person and the four layers of the person.

Husserlian phenomenology

As developed by Husserl, phenomenology is a quite technical and rigorous method focused on how we gain knowledge, and throughout his life, Husserl returned over and over to details about how the phenomenological method is to work. Stein was deeply involved in the early phenomenological school, and her first essays were written for an audience already well-versed in Husserl's texts. (It is a bit of a misnomer to call them 'essays'; none of her *Jahrbuch* publications are less than one hundred pages.) Thus, before turning to Stein's claims, it is necessary to spend a few pages on Husserl's thought and the early phenomenological school.[1]

Phenomenology has been traced as far back as the thought of Immanuel Kant (1724–1804) and G. W. F. Hegel, but certainly the key figure and arguably the founder of the more contemporary phenomenological movement is Edmund Husserl. Husserl's first studies were in mathematics and logic, and his early philosophical works investigated the philosophy of mathematics. From the publication of his two-volume work *Logical Investigations* (1900 and 1901), however, Husserl's thought centered around phenomenological concerns.

Like many late nineteenth-century thinkers, Husserl was searching for a theoretical approach that could unify all arts and sciences and a method of analysis that could reliably be applied to all fields of study. Early in her dissertation, Stein summarizes this vision and declares that the goal of phenomenology is 'to clarify and thereby to find the ultimate basis of all knowledge' (*PE*, p. 3). The dominant schools of thought against which Husserl struggled were empiricism and neo-Kantianism, or Idealism. The empiricist tradition can be traced to several key thinkers from the British Isles, especially, John Locke (1632–1704) and David Hume (1711–76), who claimed that all knowledge begins from (and, in the case of Hume, is limited to) what is gained through sense experience. They claimed that study of the empirically real world provides knowledge, and there was a celebration of the scientific method.

In contrast, the Idealist tradition, stemming from Immanuel Kant's work, insisted that the categories of consciousness or the mind are more basic than the data of our senses and, furthermore, that all sensory data are organized by and through these categories. The difference between the two traditions could perhaps be simplistically summarized with an analogy: whereas the empiricists want to gain knowledge by taking a microscope to the world, the Idealists insist that we must look at the microscope and figure out how our instrument affects the information gained through it. Kant claimed, for example, that *causality* or our understanding of events as *caused* is not a thing discoverable in the world but, rather, a category of the

21

mind used in organizing our experience. Causality (as well as space and time) is not *in* the world but is, rather, part of the structure of consciousness and 'imposed' by us upon the world. Therefore, we should investigate first and primarily these categories of mind rather than making claims about how the world is.

Husserl negotiates between these two traditions by insisting that our philosophical analyses must include both the objects of experience and experiencing subjects. He grants the Idealists' point that knowledge comes through 'instruments,' that is, through structures of our consciousnesses. He also agrees, however, with the empiricists that we must look to the world and not simply at consciousness. Husserl's 'motto,' if one may call it that, is 'to the things themselves!' (*Zu den Sachen!*), and this is understood as a focus on what *we experience*. That is, phenomenology requires one to pay attention both to the *object*, that which is experienced, and the *subject* of the experience, that to whom the experience is given.

Husserl argues that the subject experiencing and the object experienced (or, to continue our analogy, the microscope and the bug studied through the microscope) can both be best studied in conjunction by employing a descriptive method, and he regularly enjoins us to look carefully at our experience and study how things are given to us. A common German phrase is '*es gibt*,' which literally translated would be 'it gives,' but is equivalent to the English phrase 'there is'. Drawing from this German phrase, phenomenologists often talk of what is given and the givenness of things, and the term 'phenomenon' refers to that which is given immediately to us or that which we experience first-hand. (Kant made a clear distinction between the *phenomenal* and *noumenal* realms, or 'mere appearances' and the things as they are in themselves. Phenomenology makes no such distinction, and 'phenomena' in phenomenology are not opposed to noumena.)

Husserl argues that both the Idealists and empiricists have misunderstood our experience and thereby our knowledge. Contra the empiricists, we must consider the way our consciousness and the structures of our consciousness affect our experience. There are never raw sense data; there is always *someone* who experiences and senses the data, someone to whom they are given. But Husserl is not happy simply studying consciousness; consciousness is always directed toward things. We are not subjects standing over against and separate from objects, but subjects involved in, interested in, and in concourse with things. Because all experience is the experience of a subject or ego in relation to some object, we must study them together and rightly understand how those things are given to us.

Thus, the phenomenological method is most properly a description of phenomena, and the goal is an accurate description of our experience. While rational argument, internal coherence and consistency are not insignificant, the paradigmatic court of appeal in phenomenology is each person's experience. In her phenomenological writings Stein gives us descriptions that she expects each reader to test against his or her own experience. They are not primarily arguments *per se* but descriptions, the evidence for which lies within our own immediate experience. (Among the criticisms of Stein's later philosophical work is the claim that she gave up the aims of phenomenology in incorporating revealed truths, the Incarnation, the Trinity, etc., in the development of – and perhaps in the support of (?) – her philosophical positions.)

Phenomenology saw itself as fundamental to all other disciplines insofar as it is necessary to be clear about what the phenomena in question are prior to analyzing any other aspect of them. If one wants, for example, to ask about the proper method for teaching the Socratic *elenchus*, one should first become clear about what it means to teach, and how teaching differs from preaching or spreading propaganda or merely chatting with friends. Similarly, if one is engaged in the natural sciences, one must first become clear about what distinguishes the natural sciences from the social sciences or humanities. Husserl argued that only through phenomenology, with its focus on pure descriptions of essential structures, is there a basis upon which to study accurately anything else, including the objects of the other sciences.

Thus, the primary aim of phenomenology is to give adequate attention to the phenomena, that is, to our experiences. In order to do so, however, Husserl insists that we need to be wary of preconceptions, prejudices and inherited interpretations which prevent a pure access to the phenomena. Such preconceptions and assumptions may lead us to think we understand something, rather than looking to the experience itself. Further, if the phenomenological analysis is to be foundational, it cannot depend upon previous analysis. Any reliance on tradition or traditional philosophical interpretations, models or premises is problematic. Instead, Husserl wants to begin anew in order to gain genuine and reliable insight into the objects of our experience. Thus, the phrase 'to the things themselves!' refers not only to the method of turning to the phenomena of experience, but also to the insistence that solutions are not to be discovered through study of the writings of others but through a direct confrontation with the philosophical problems themselves.

The first steps of phenomenological analysis include the intuition, analysis, and description of some phenomenon, for example, of joy or empathetic understanding. Phenomenological descriptions aim at providing guideposts for others to enable them to understand and grasp more clearly the phenomena in question. Yet to communicate all of one's experience to another would prove both exhausting and, quite likely, uninteresting. Therefore, the works aim not at a comprehensive description of the experience but, rather, at the grasping of the *essence* of some experience. For example, using one of Stein's favorite examples, one may analyze the experience of joy. In so doing, the phenomenologist would need to delimit some particular experience of joy and analyze it in order to discover what is essential to joy as such, what distinguishes joy from mere giddiness, relief, euphoria, contentment, etc. An analysis of the essence of joy searches for those traits or structures that make any joyful experience an experience of joy and not of something else.

Central to the phenomenological method as employed by Husserl and Stein is the focus on *essences*, and Stein retains the phenomenological concern for essential structures throughout all of her writings, making it the lynchpin of her rapprochement between medieval philosophy and phenomenology. Further, the claims regarding essences provided a clear challenge to the empiricist schools of the day. The empiricists claimed that all that exists are particular entities – the maple tree out back and my memory of yesterday's basketball game. These are things that can be grasped through particular sensory experiences. But if the empiricists are right, then it is not clear how we can make any general or universal claims (there would be nothing common to my joyful experience and my friend's joyful moment such that I could confidently say 'all joy is …'). Likewise, logical laws would turn out to be generalizations, much like the laws of the natural sciences. Just as a law in physics is derived from repeated experiments resulting in the predicted conclusion, so logical laws (for example, that A cannot both be and not be in the same respect at the same time) would also be the result of the frequent recurrence of the same result and could be, at best, highly probable.

Husserl challenged this conclusion by arguing that we have access to essences or structures that are identical in more than one instance and foundational for that experience. Once one understands an essential structure, one grasps what must be the case anytime that kind of thing occurs; an essence is that which makes a thing to be that kind of thing. If there are such structures, then our thinking does not develop the laws of logic or universals but is, rather, regulated by them.

We come to grasp essences through, what Husserl calls, *eidetic intuition*, and he prescribes various methods for achieving this insight. In *Logical Investigations* and *Ideas I*, Husserl lays out two methods, the eidetic reduction and the epoche or transcendental reduction, intended to help us reach the point where we have rid ourselves sufficiently of our presuppositions so that we may accurately study the phenomenon. The first reduction, the eidetic reduction, involves the elimination of all accidental aspects of the phenomenon in order to discover the essence of that phenomenon. One begins by choosing some particular example, perhaps a particular joyful experience. Then one varies the example imaginatively until the essential structure is discovered. For example, we could imagine numerous variations of my present joyful experience, changing the time, the conditions, the content of the news motivating my joy, my own physical state, etc. These variations alter the experience (in our imaginations) until the essential structure of joy is discovered and we are able to recognize any genuine experience of joy as having that structure.

The second method, the epoche, draws from the work of René Descartes (1596–1650). In both the *Meditations on First Philosophy* and the *Discourse on Method*, Descartes recommends a method of thinking that will, he insists, lead to indubitable knowledge. Judgments regarding what and how something exists are subject to deception (we could be dreaming or there might be an evil genius deceiving us), but what we experience cannot be so doubted. That there is a cat before me is dubious; that I *think* there is a cat before me is not. Husserl begins from this Cartesian insight in developing the phenomenological epoche – although attempting to develop a method slightly less radical than Descartes'. (Husserl recommends simply bracketing claims regarding existence rather than denying them.)

Both methods are intended to help us focus our attention on the essential structures of the phenomena in question, bracketing all judgments, preconceptions and assumptions so that we can have a clear and precise understanding of the structures in question. Herbert Spiegelberg, in his text on the phenomenological movement, says that, although this task may seem in theory like 'a fairly elementary affair ... it is certainly not so in practice.'[2] Husserl dedicated much of his career to clarifying details of the method, and his life's labors were spent on describing ever more precisely how consciousness works. Husserl was convinced that a right understanding of how we come to know anything is critical for intellectual pursuits of any kind.

Stein's phenomenology

Stein's first phenomenological project in her dissertation follows, in large measure, this procedure; she insists that only once we know *what* empathy is (that is, the essence of empathy) can we ask whether and how such things occur. Yet, while Stein appears to accept the epoche or transcendental reduction in a number of places, especially in her dissertation, in the end she rejects the transcendental project, insisting instead on a realist phenomenology. She was clearly worried that there may be idealistic tendencies in the transcendental reduction, and she speaks briefly in her autobiographical writings of an ongoing feud with the 'Master' over this issue:

> [t]he *Logical Investigations* had caused a sensation primarily because it appeared to be a radical departure from critical idealism which had a Kantian and neo-Kantian stamp. It was considered a 'new scholasticism' because it turned attention away from the 'subject' and toward 'things' themselves. Perception again appeared as reception, deriving its laws from objects not, as criticism has it, from determination which imposes its laws on the objects. All the young phenomenologists were confirmed realists. However, the *Ideas* included some expressions which sounded very much as though their Master wished to return to idealism. Nor could his oral interpretation dispel our misgivings. (*Life*, p. 250, translation adapted slightly)

Throughout his career, Husserl lost many disciples who refused to follow various turns in his explication of the phenomenological method. Stein accepts the *Logical Investigations* quite unambiguously, but refuses to fully endorse *Ideas I* or the subsequent publications that develop the transcendental reduction. Instead, she identifies herself with the tradition of phenomenological realism. (Proponents of phenomenological realism include the influential Max Scheler, Stein's teacher Adolf Reinach, her close friends Hedwig Conrad-Martius and Roman Ingarden, and another Polish thinker, Karol Wojtyła [Pope John Paul II].)

Realist phenomenologists are characterized by a rejection of the transcendental reduction and its attempt to bracket claims regarding existence. In contrast, the realist school claims that such bracketing (and all appeals to doubt, error, and hallucination) only makes sense in the context of a general acceptance of the existence of the world and our veridical awareness of that world. Individual experiences or objects may turn out to be dubious, erroneous, or illusory, but only against the backdrop of an awareness of the truly existing world. Our consciousness is always already involved with objects and existing entities, and any attempt to reach a purified consciousness (that is, purified of all 'prejudices' concerning existence and dedicated solely to the study of ideal structures) must fail.[3]

Although critical of some aspects of the Husserlian project, Stein was nonetheless attracted both by the rigor of phenomenology and by its promise to offer a more adequate foundation for claims in all areas, including her own original area of study, psychology. While in Göttingen, Stein became deeply involved in the phenomenological circle, and for her dissertation, she chose a topic of great interest to Husserl: empathy.

Empathy

Phenomenology is dedicated to the analysis of experiences, and Stein, in analyzing empathy, studied a particular kind of experience – that of *our* experience of *another's* experience. Despite, however, the title, *On the Problem of Empathy*, the book is only partially about our sensitivity to the feelings of others, or 'empathy' as commonly used in English. In the process of describing the essential structure of empathy, Stein also addresses more technical questions in phenomenology, including a central problem in the phenomenological method. Husserlian phenomenology begins with that which is immediate and certain, our own consciousness; however, viewing ourselves as monadic centers isolated from others is simply not an adequate description of our experience. We do not find ourselves isolated, solipsistic centers of consciousness, but involved in a world filled with other people and other centers of consciousness. The question then arises of how we should understand our relation, knowledge, and involvement with others. Thus, Stein's study of empathy concerns not simply empathy as one kind of experience, but also how the phenomenological project itself should be conceived: should we understand experience as *my* experience of the world or as *our* encounter with the world?[4]

27

In the first part of the text, Stein presents an eidetic analysis of empathy and, in the second, develops her understanding of the human being and our structure, such that we can have empathetic experiences. Stein describes empathy through an analogy with other mental acts such as memory, anticipation, and fantasy. In each of these cases, the *act* is immediately experienced (that is, I now remember, anticipate, or fantasize) but the *content* is not (that is, what is remembered, anticipated, or fantasized is not now present). Hamlet might, for example, remember his experience of his father's ghost, and through the memory, he (re-)experiences something that happened to him at a previous time. Hamlet does not re-experience the event in the sense that he goes back in time to the original event but in the sense that the same content is re-activated, although always as a memory of an event now past. In the same way, in empathetic experiences, we experience something, some content or event, and relive that content, but always as something not now occurring to us but as another's experience. The experience that we have is primordial and first-hand; the content, however, is not – just as the content of Hamlet's memory is not primordial. Thus, memory and empathy work in a similar way: we now experience what we can no longer (in the case of memory) or could never (in the case of empathy) experience primordially. But the present experience 'announces' another experience, in the case of Hamlet, that he had seen his father's ghost, or in the case of empathy, that my friend is sad.

Stein places the distinction between the *act of experiencing* and the *content experienced* at the center of her discussion of empathy. (This distinction is also employed in other places. For example, in *Philosophy of Psychology and the Humanities*, Stein uses it in order to account for 'sham emotions,' that is, intense experiences of non-intense contents and thus a stronger experience than the content seems to warrant.) She also develops in some detail three basic phases that all empathized experiences undergo. In so doing, Stein is interested in articulating what it means to empathize another's experience. She insists that we do not *infer* how another feels (from facial experiences, context or actions), nor do we *conjecture* or *project* ourselves into the other (in the sense that we suppress the other and appropriate her experience). Instead, we experience the same content that the other undergoes in a first-hand way and thereby have access to the inner life of another in a way that is not dependent on our ability to guess well. This is not to say that we have indubitable or exhaustive access to another's experiences, although in the ideal case the empathized experience is identical in content with the original experience (although different in its mode of givenness). Empathy is thus a two-sided experience: it is both our own and announces an experience that is not, and has never been, our own.

Empathy is central to the phenomenological project, and, Stein argues, empathetic experiences are also central to being a person. Throughout her dissertation, we can see arguments for the thesis that we cannot understand or know ourselves without relationships with others (see, for example, *On the Problem of Empathy* [*PE* p. 88]). And she presents at least two ways in which other people are necessary for self-knowledge. First, it is through the other's perception of me as an 'object' to be seen, understood (to some degree), and evaluated that I am able to do so for myself. Through the other's perception of me, I become real to myself. We can think of someone experiencing hallucinations. That person can only recognize certain experiences as hallucinatory because other people treat the hallucinated objects as unreal. Unless she sees the other treating some objects as real and others as non-existent, she cannot herself distinguish which is which. Because we have access to others' experiences, we see certain things as shared, that is, as real.

In the second chapter of her dissertation, Stein discusses the reiteration of empathy, that is, where one empathizes another's empathetic experiences. For example, I may understand that another takes joy in my joy, or I may be comforted by my friend's empathetic understanding of my grief. It is through such empathy and reiterated empathy that we come to share a world and recognize our own inner experiences as real. Thus, Stein argues that I cannot see myself or my own experiences as part of the world until I have experienced another so understanding me.

Similarly, it is only when another sees me as an 'object' that I have the consequent ability to do so myself. This ability to see ourselves as objects and 'stand back' from ourselves, allows us to evaluate and decide what kind of people we want to become and, therefore, how we should act. It is the condition of our freedom. Additionally, Stein points out that, at times, another person may reveal our own nature to us more truthfully than we perceive it ourselves. Stein gives the example: while I may think that I act out of pure generosity, another person may notice that I look around for approval after doing some kindness (see *PE*, Chapter 3, §5p).

Stein offers a second role for empathy in self-knowledge: what the other does informs me of what I may become. Potentialities are that which can be, but are not yet. As such, they are hidden. If, however, I see another act courageously before a group of peers or colleagues, I may recognize the yet-unrealized potential for courage in myself. The other, thus, both allows me an objectivity toward myself necessary for truly free actions and 'informs' me of the possibilities or potentialities among which I may choose. Because we develop, and because our knowledge of ourselves and our potentialities is incomplete, other people, Stein insists, are necessary even to be ourselves. (In an appendix added to her 1936 work *Finite and Eternal Being*, Stein reiterates the claim that the understanding of ourselves is enabled through contact with others, but then she adds that grace too is necessary. Although empathetic experiences are foundational for our self-knowledge, 'many sources of error are bound with this knowledge which remains hidden from us so long as God does not, through a genuine interior shock – through a *call* in the interior – take the bandages, which cover the interior of each human being in a special way, from our eyes.')[5] Empathy is a key part of self-knowledge, and Stein further employs her understanding of empathy in order to distinguish motivation and causality.

Causality and motivation

In both her dissertation and subsequent contributions to Husserl's *Jahrbuch*, Stein describes each individual as an entity capable of empathetic experiences, that is, capable of following along the experience of another and thus understanding the experiences of another.[6] The *Jahrbuch* essays, however, articulate more fully how and to what degree we have access to the experiences of others. The first *Jahrbuch* essay, translated as 'Sentient Causality,' was completed in 1919, two years before her conversion, and published with her second essay in the 1922 *Jahrbuch*. In these articles, as she presents her phenomenological analysis of the person, Stein also challenges a number of popular theories of human action, including determinism and indeterminism.

Determinists claim that all human actions are fully determined and, because of that, no human being can act freely. They claim that every state, 'whatever it may be, is determined unambiguously by the series of preceding states and is calculable from them' ('Sentient Causality' in *Philosophy of Psychology and the Humanities* [*PPHi*], p. 32). This position has gained increasing influence with the rise of science and materialism, and determinists use the model of the physical sciences in order to understand human actions. As a billiard ball will move in a predictable way given the direction and momentum of the cue ball which bumps it, so also human actions can be precisely predicted if we have sufficient information about the forces acting upon our bodies and psyches. The determinists claim that just as physical events are fully causally determined, so human actions are fully causally determined.

In contrast, indeterminists insist on human freedom, but they do so by claiming that some actions are uncaused. Indeterminism attempts to preserve human freedom by denying that all events are caused – some, they say, are exempt from causal determination and thus can be free. But the question then arises: if an action has no cause, can it be understood? It is not clear that the indeterminists can give an adequate answer to this, and thus they preserve human freedom at the expense of the intelligibility of free acts. One can no more understand free actions, as described by the indeterminists, than one can understand a 'chance occurrence.'

Stein accepts neither the determinist nor the indeterminist thesis fully, but instead she uses a phenomenological description of human actions in order to distinguish different kinds of relations among acts, delimiting the realm of freedom and that of causal relations. Her method for overcoming what she sees as inadequate positions is a more thorough and careful description of the phenomena.

Much of the essay 'Sentient Causality' is dedicated to making careful distinctions, and the primary one that Stein makes is between *causality* and *motivation*. She develops this distinction by looking at human actions, and she provides phenomenological descriptions of inclining, willing, affirming, adopting, acknowledging, and other mental attitudes and actions. Through this analysis, she pinpoints what is specific to free actions and the attitude of will that characterizes genuinely free acts. As Stein presents it, the characteristic of free acts is that, while they are motivated and therefore intelligible, they are not caused and thus can arise from a personal *fiat*. Stein understands causal relations as necessary connections between events (for example, there is a necessary relation between plucking a string in a certain way and the resulting tone). In contrast, motivation is a rational, but not a necessary, connection between two acts (for example, the progression of the chords played: chords of a certain variety *motivate* completion in a certain way, but one could simply refuse to finish a song).

Relations of motivation are, according to Stein, connections of meaning. She describes them as 'an *emerging* of the one *out of* the other, a self fulfilling or being fulfilled of the one *on the basis of* the other *for the sake of* the other' (*PPH*i, p. 41). Motivated acts arise on the basis of previous states of affairs or for the sake of some future state of affairs, but motivated acts – in contrast to caused acts – are not necessary. The perceptual experience of the color red may motivate belief in the existence of the red object, but I need not thereby believe in its existence (as Husserl's transcendental reduction shows us). The steps of a mathematical proof motivate the acceptance of the conclusion, but they do not *necessitate* the acceptance of the conclusion (as wrong answers of numerous students show).

Further, in some cases of motivation, there may be several possible conclusions. There might, for example, be a number of ways to complete a musical phrase (in contrast to a problem in mathematics), all of which sound melodious. Stein claims that '[o]ne state of affairs can enter into quite different logical connections and, correspondingly, authorize many claims.' Nonetheless, 'it defines a range of possibilities, and if the knowing subject departs from this range, it proceeds irrationally' (*PPH*i, p. 44). A motive may *permit* a range of behaviors without requiring any one of them. Stein insists that:

> [m]otivation is a *coherence of meaning* in which experiences cannot coincide *randomly*. On the basis of any specific motive, various actions might be conceivable; yet by that fact a range of possibilities is defined and they alone obtain for any individual – regardless of the rest of the circumstances. (*PPH*i, p. 94)

Thus, a motivational set-up does not predict which behaviors must arise, but which ones *can*, and motivation is intimately tied to the phenomenological theory of essences and essential relations (insofar as the essential structure prescribes what can and cannot be the case while the thing remains that kind of thing).

Stein describes causality as a '*blind occurring*,' whereas motiv-ation is an '*insightful doing*' (*PPH*i, p. 46). Relations of motivation are intelligible and stand under rational laws. Furthermore, the motivations of others are available to me through empathy, whereas causal relations, because they are 'blind' occurrences, are not. One understands motivated sequences through empathy, through feeling into an experience and having insight into the sequence of acts. One understands causal sequences, in contrast, by subtracting motiv-ations until one is left with the unintelligible yet predictable patterns.

The person

This distinction between causality and motivation is not in itself new. Stein clearly drew parts of it from her work on Husserl's manuscripts. However, in addition to distinguishing causality and motivation, she insists that the two overlap. This can best be seen through her theory of the person. Stein claims that there are four phenomenological layers, or ways of accessing our experience, in each human being. The layers are distinct, but they also, within the individual, affect each other. Further, there are 'laws' appropriate to each layer, although what occurs in one layer will have implications and resonate within the other three. The layers are: the physical, the sentient (*psychische*), the mental (*geistige*), and the personal. (Unfortunately, several key terms are translated differently in the dissertation, translated by Waltraut Stein, and *Philosophy of Psychology and the Humanities* [*PPH*], translated by Mary Catharine Baseheart and Marianne Sawicki. Most notable among these are *psychische* ['psychic' in *PE*, 'sentient' in *PPH*] and *geistige* ['spiritual' in *PE*, 'mental' in *PPH*]. I will be following Baseheart's and Sawicki's choices in the following discussion.) These levels should not be thought of as distinct spatial locations but, rather, indicate the ways in which phenomena register within an individual.

We can contrast the four layers or realms: the physical is primarily our physical body, and the sentient layer is built upon the physical body. Sentience, however, is not identical with our physical matter but is, rather, the living body. We can see this in the difference between cutting a finger and the involuntary response to the pain. The spontaneous jump is not identical with the physical event, but arises from and is related to the physical event. The mental is the layer of meaning and intellectual thought, and the personal is the realm of freedom and the personal core. It is, most properly, the *person*.

We can see these four layers in action by developing the previous example. Suppose that I slice my finger with a knife while preparing a salad. The cut itself occurs on the physical level. When I register the event a few moments later as I see blood glistening on the blade of the knife, I gasp and shudder quickly. The cut has registered on the sentient level. I may then think to myself, 'Sarah, you knew that this knife was too sharp to use for this, and especially when you are in a hurry.' I would thus register the event on the mental level, making intelligible how and why the event occurred. And, finally, I might make the free decision to sit for a minute, calm myself down, find a bandage, and continue making dinner with a different knife. The final decisions were not necessary ones – I could have cried and abandoned the meal – but rather free decisions arising from the personal realm.

Sigmund Freud (1856–1939) was developing his psychoanalytic method when Stein wrote her phenomenological essays, and it is unlikely that she was familiar with his works. Nonetheless, in an apparent case of parallel development, Stein develops a concept of *lifepower* that has similarities with Freud's *libido*. According to Stein, the sentient level is ruled by lifepower, which she understands as an enduring property of all living sentient beings, a kind of continuous power that has influxes and outflows. All of our experiences 'cost' us a certain amount of lifepower; likewise, other experiences may 'feed' us lifepower. Lifepower appears to be a causally regulated force, and everything in the current of conscious experience is conditioned by this lifepower. (Stein refers to its causal determination as *sensate causality*, that is, causality in our sensate states, rather than our physical ones.)

In her descriptions of lifepower, Stein appears to have in mind an analogy with electricity. (The newest technology in her day would have included the electrical current and electromagnetic radiation.[7]) Just as a refrigerator is run on a constant current of electricity, so our life requires a current of lifepower. Our level or amount of lifepower, however, may rise and fall, depending upon what is using up and what is feeding the steam of lifepower, and we can see the conditioning of lifepower in our daily activities. For example, if I am well and have a full supply of lifepower, I may be struck by the blueness of the sky and have an intense experience of its beauty; whereas on a day when my lifepower reserves are low, I may have but a weak experience of the same blue color. Likewise, if one's lifepower is ebbing, she may be unable to feel in a way appropriate to a situation; she might, for example, fail to be joyful at the arrival of good news. In such cases, one understands that the situation is a joyous one and even desires to be joyful but nonetheless fails to feel joy. (Stein spends a good deal of time analyzing cases endemic to scholars: she points to experiences of indeterminate restlessness, the inability to concentrate, or the impulse to go on a recreational trip rather than work.[8] Such situations, she argues, point to the causal conditioning of our feelings and mental acts by our lifepower supply.)

All experiences draw on our lifepower resources, but they make fewer demands on that source as one gets used to them. For example, when someone first arrives in New York City or London, especially if he is from a smaller town, the city may be overwhelming and exhausting. But as he gets used to the city, spending the day in Manhattan or negotiating the underground simply takes less energy and makes fewer demands on his lifepower. Thus, we can change the degree to which certain experiences draw from the lifepower by developing a 'faculty' or habit for such experiences. Every experience, however, requires lifepower, and these faculties take time in order to develop. (In several of her letters, Stein advises the recipient to live simply in order to have the energy to dedicate to prayer. Although not explicitly using the language of her philosophical work, her words contain the warning that even small tasks and choices draw from the lifepower reserves and can take away from our more important tasks.)

Stein argues that causality rules the physical and sentient layers of the individual, and lifepower functions according to causal laws. In contrast, motivation functions on the level of meaning, and meaning rules the third level: the mental realm. At the threshold between the sentient and mental levels, however, meanings can convert into lifepower and lifepower into meaning.[9] For example, through reading a book or studying a painting one may find oneself energized. Stein explains this by claiming that the meaning found in the work of art can be converted into sentient lifepower. (Neither the book nor the painting are exhausted through my enjoyment of them. Meaning, unlike lifepower, is not directly subject to causal laws, and thus works of art contribute a more lasting source of lifepower to a community than other physical or sentient sources of energy.) This conversion of meaning and lifepower explains phenomena such as an individual's ability to continue a task far beyond her physical and sentient resources when she has a sense of purpose, but the relative ease with which the same person may be drained when working at some rote task. The meaning of the task converts directly into sentient energy and feeds a system that otherwise would be easily sapped by the work. Thus, Stein understands the lifepower circuit, not as a closed system, but as one affected by outside sources: art, music, and nature can feed and replenish lifepower supplies in a way analogous to physical rest, and, although written before her baptism, Stein also suggests that there may be supernatural sources of lifepower.

Influences flow directly between the physical and the sentient realms and between the sentient and the mental realms. In addition, Stein claims that the fourth realm, the personal layer, retains its own reserve of lifepower regardless of the state of the other three realms.

The fourth realm, the center of the will, always has the power to make a resolve, even though the physical, sentient, and mental reserves may be low or exhausted. The personal realm, Stein claims, is properly the center of the person and the center of free choices, and, although conditioned by sentient causality and directed by motives, it nonetheless retains its distinctness. The personal realm is not utterly independent of the other levels (they provide conditioning influences); it is nonetheless relatively independent. Thus, it is – contra the determinists – impossible to predict human actions. The level of lifepower affects our choices, and motives guide our impulses, but the person must *choose* which motive to follow, and she always retains the power to direct her *fiat*. Stein says, '[h]ow any one decision of the will is going to turn out cannot be predicted either on the basis of a thorough survey of the motivational framework or from knowledge of the available lifepower' (*PPH*i, p. 96). Decisions are not automatic; they do not follow the 'weightier' motive, as a scale tips to the heavier side. Rather, we must decide that a motive is weightier and choose that motive through a *fiat* of the will. Free actions certainly presuppose a motive, but a motive is not in itself sufficient. There must also be in every free choice an impulse that it is not itself motivated.

Stein agrees with the determinists that there are causal factors in all human actions, but she insists that these are not determining of human actions, but only conditioning of them. In contrast to the indeterminists, she insists that free acts are not simply uncaused. Rather, they are motivated and, thus, intelligible. A motive, however, is not in itself sufficient for a free action. The motive must be chosen through an impulse of will, and no motive is determinative for the will. In exploring the four phenomenological layers of the person, the personal layer, however, is crucial for understanding the uniqueness of each individual.

The personal layer

In each individual, there are, Stein claims, four levels at which we register experiences, and the fourth, the personal layer, is the center for our free acts. The personal layer is not, however, simply a will devoid of all character. Rather, each individual is marked with a unique personality.

In all her writings at each stage of her career, Stein repeats the claim that each individual has a personal core which is unique to that individual and which characterizes the person and all of her actions.

36

We could use a botanical image: as a flower opens itself to the sun, so the core of the person opens itself out in our thoughts and actions (although it is not reducible to our thoughts and actions). This personal core resides most properly in the personal layer, although its influence reverberates through all the layers.

In her dissertation, Stein says: we can think of Caesar, for example, in a village or in Rome, in the twentieth century or in the first, and certainly 'his historically settled individuality would then go through some changes' but, nonetheless, 'just as surely he would remain Caesar' (*PE*, p. 110). There is, she says, in each person a core or personal structure that 'marks off a range of possibilities of variation within which the person's real distinctiveness can be developed "ever according to circumstances"' (ibid.). That is, each of us has a personal structure that is determinate for our personality. The circumstances in which we live – for example, Caesar living in a village rather than in Rome – will certainly impact on our development and the choices available to us. But it does not affect our fundamental personality. Regardless of where Caesar lives or under what conditions, certain traits and potentialities will be identical. These are rooted in his personal core.

Because the personal core has a kind of permanence, it is not 'trainable' and cannot be developed. Thus, she says that one cannot educate the person (here she is referring to the personal layer, not the individual as a whole). We may more and less *realize* or *unfold* the core, but the core itself does not change. She says:

> [a]ny work on yourself, any efforts toward a cleansing of your soul can consist only in this: to suppress negatively valued deeds and stirrings of your soul and to combat the disposition to them, or even not to let them arise, and conversely to hold yourself open for positive values. But you can neither instill the qualities of your soul into yourself nor break yourself of them. If a change enters into this sphere, then it's not the occurrence of a 'development,' but rather is to be regarded as a transformation through an 'other-worldly' power, that is, a power situated outside of the person and outside of all [*sic*] natural connections in which she is entangled. ('Individual and Community' in *Philosophy of Psychology and the Humanities* [*PPH*ii], pp. 232–3)

Stein is *not* claiming that we cannot develop habits or dispositions. She is, however, claiming that aptitudes or *pre*dispositions cannot be developed. The aptitudes themselves – for example, the gift for mathematical thinking – cannot be developed, but one can gain (or refuse to learn) information about mathematics and practice will make doing equations easier. While we may develop the habits and dispositions (or allow them to sit stagnant), the aptitudes and predispositions underlying those can only be changed by a supernatural, otherworldly transformation.

We can see this idea developed in her later spiritual writings. For example, in the *Hidden Life*, Stein briefly speaks of an internal and individual structure longing for self-expression that cannot freely unfold without assistance but is so individual that merely importing images from outside ourselves is inappropriate. Rather, each individual is unique, and in importing foreign models, one may squash her own positive individual traits and character. Stein claims that this form is deeply hidden and needs divine help in order to unfold; she says, 'this inner shaping power that is in bondage strains toward a light that will guide more surely, and a power that will free it and give it space. This is the light and the power of divine grace' (*The Hidden Life: Essays, Meditations, Spiritual Texts* [*HL*], p. 28). And in a work from the mid 1930s, *Finite and Eternal Being*, Stein sees in each person an 'unrepeatable mirror of God in his soul' (*Endliches und ewiges Sein* [EeS], p. 473). The uniqueness of each person reflects another 'face' of God, and the varieties of unique souls are a 'garland' adding to the beauty and variety of creation.[10]

Stein insists that each of us has a unique personal core that characterizes us and is permanent, abiding unchanged throughout our lives under any and all circumstances. It does, however, unfold and imprint our actions and lives ever more deeply. We could return to the image of the flower. Just as a flower begins closed and only gradually opens to the sun, so our personal core begins tucked within itself and only gradually blooms out in our mental, sentient, and physical life. In Chapter 2, §3c of 'Individual and Community,' Stein offers a warning and striking images for the different ways in which we may deny our soul or personal core: we may fail to be 'awake' or suppress, or even deny, our own distinctiveness. Such a life becomes empty, rigid, and dry.

The personal layer is home to the personal core and to our will. In addition, the personal layer is open to the world of value. Stein's theory of value was clearly influenced by the thought of Max Scheler, who claimed that human beings do not aspire to pleasure or to any emotional state, but rather to values. If we aim for pleasure, we do so only because we believe that it is valuable. Likewise, our emotions – our love, hatred, approval, disapproval, shame, and joy –

are all motivated by the perception of value. (We could contrast this claim with, for example, the psychoanalytic claim that desire originates in the loss of the first object, the mother, or David Hume's claim that desires are prior to all rational or cognitive acts.) Like Scheler, Stein insists that our emotions are responses to values. One does not simply feel in a particular way, but feels that way *because* she takes the object of the emotion to have a certain value. In *On the Problem of Empathy*, she contrasts grief at the death of a friend with the grief experienced at the discovery that one who you thought was a friend was not worthy of your esteem. In the first case, the grief is real and deep, but with the friend's death the value of the friend is neither lost nor diminished. But in the second case, although the individual is still alive, the value attributed to her is lost, a loss greater than that of death.

Stein argues, as Scheler did, that values have an objective hierarchy and that the level at which a value is felt can be evaluated. If someone feels a greater grief at the loss of a scientific manuscript than at the loss of a friend, then the person has misunderstood the value of each and her emotional reactions indicate a distortion. Development as a person includes the formation of a rightly ordered value hierarchy, and such formation *is* the development of right emotional responses to value. Values, Stein insists, require certain attitudes, not in the sense that they *cause* those attitudes or feelings, but in the sense that they *motivate* them; they are rationally required. We cannot 'see' certain values without feeling them. For example, if a certain landscape leaves me cold, then I have not seen its beauty. Thus, one cannot separate our comprehension of value from our emotional response to that value.

Our personalities, Stein claims, are due more to the susceptibility one has to different values and the way in which that is acted out in practice than to properties such as a good memory, a clear understanding, or attunement to sensory details. We are not characterized primarily by our intellectual talents and capacities, but by the way in which we value things. By this, she does not mean simply that one is characterized by her moral qualities or actions *per se* but, rather, that one is characterized by her 'permeability for value in general': 'we see what the person *is* when we see which world of value she lives in, which values she is responsive to, and what achievements she may be creating, prompted by values' (*PPH*ii, p. 227). Therefore, the actions themselves are not as revealing of the person as an understanding of the emotional attunement to the values motivating the actions.

39

Different personality 'types' can be understood in terms of the way in which people of those types feel values. For example, a scientific type is one who is especially sensitive to knowledge and the pursuit of knowledge (although perhaps less so to people). Stein insists that the ideal person is one who has all his feelings in the appropriate hierarchy and has adequate feelings that 'correspond to the entire realm of value levels' (*PE*, p. 108). All types are an 'abolition of certain value ranges' (ibid.). But typing people is possible because people often value in characteristic ways, all of which proximate yet nonetheless fall short of the ideal. (These failings cannot be seen merely as an accident of our lives. We must also *open* ourselves up to value. It does not simply permeate us, but requires an active reception. Thus, a failure to value properly is also a failure to be appropriately receptive to a real value.)

According to Stein, emotions are the feeling of values and, thus, are 'closer' to the person than thoughts or sensory experiences.[11] The response to value is, in fact, 'the "most natural" behavior for the person' (*PPH*ii, p. 227). It is not our thoughts which reveal most intimately our person, but our affective life. (Stein does distinguish emotional disturbances which do not issue from the 'core' and in which 'your soul is not implicated' from affective responses to value properly speaking [*PPH*ii, p. 229]. I take the former to include depression, anxiety or other emotional states resulting from physical or chemical imbalances.) And the soul, she says, is 'at home' in the world of value.

In *Logical Investigations*, Husserl discusses relations of *intentionality* and *fulfillment*. (I will address this topic in more detail in Chapter 6 below. See the section on her theory of knowledge, pp. 113–15.) Phenomenology is dedicated to the study of phenomena, that is, that which appears to us. But what appears to us, always appears *as* something. Husserl insists that all experiences are intended as some kind or another; I never experience simply sensations, but always experience them as having some structure. The white furry mess on the floor is experienced *as* my cat or *as* a towel left on the floor. In studying phenomena, one studies not simply the experiential data 'in its purity,' but the ways in which we constitute or understand that data. *Intentions* and *intentionality*, in the Husserlian sense, refer to the ways in which we understand a given phenomenon. For example, I may interpret a pair of overalls, plaid shirt, and straw hat standing in the field *as* a scarecrow. The intention of my perception is the notion of 'scarecrow' through which I understand my perceptual experience. It may turn out, however, that upon closer inspection, my intention is not fulfilled, and I discover that, instead of a stuffed scarecrow standing in the field, the figure is the farmer himself.

Husserl claims that all knowledge is a relation between our intentions and their various fulfillments (or corrections). Stein furthers this claim by insisting that all intentions of objects (for example, seeing the figure in the field *as* a scarecrow) include value intentions. One cannot, she says, intend or constitute an object as something (as a scarecrow or as a farmer) without also understanding it as having a certain value (as a thing that can be hit if one is forced off the road, or as a human being whose life is to be preserved). Value is coextensive with the physical world and, Stein claims, just as real. She says, '[a] value-constitution goes hand in hand with every object-constitution. Every fully constituted object is simultaneously a value-object' (*PPH*ii, p. 160). Thus, I cannot understand my sensory experience as a farmer or as a scarecrow without also attributing to those objects some kind of value.

The idea of a 'value-free world of mere things' is, thus, an abstraction arising from a certain 'orientation,' that is, an orientation that limits the ways in which we are aware of our experiences of objects. One can only think of the world as without value by eliminating or ignoring large parts of our experience. What is dropped out in order to come up with a 'value-free world' is our emotional life. Stein argues that the primary way in which we gain awareness of values is through our feelings and affective responses, and if one perceives the world as without value, she has only done so by failing to be aware of her affective experience or by being blind to objects to such a degree that she fails to be affected by them. These affective and volitional aspects of the individual personality are intertwined with the other three phenomenal layers.

The four layers in relation to others

Thus, the individual, as understood by Stein, is 'composed' of four phenomenal layers, each of which permeates the others. The center of the individual, however, lies in the personal layer, the home of the personal core, the will, and our affective life. Each individual has direct access to her own phenomenal layers, yet we can also receive phenomena from others, and there is real access and interaction between individuals. Interpersonal relations and knowledge of other persons occurs directly through the mental level and secondarily through the sentient layer. We have an openness to the mental and sentient life of others that differs fundamentally from our understanding of their physical and personal life. Stein claims that '[s]ince this openness belongs to the original lifestyle of the mental individual, you can rightly say that the individual's essence is just as originally social as individual' (*PPH*ii, p. 296). While we cannot experience the cut to another's flesh, we do wince and feel a bit sick when she is cut. We have access to and can follow part of the experience of another even though we do not share her flesh. Likewise, we have access to the motivational chains and reasoning processes of others. I can understand and follow along the reasons a friend gives for marrying a particular man; I have access to the coherence and rationality of her choice.

Despite this access, however, there is not complete access. Both the physical and the personal levels of each individual are inaccessible in any direct way to others. It can easily be seen that the physical layer is not accessible: what happens to my own body happens in this place, to this flesh; no one else can have access in a first-person way to my flesh. Likewise, the personal level is opaque. This layer includes our will, the *fiat* that decides. While others can attempt to influence, exploit, convince, and persuade, it is ultimately up to each person whether she accepts and acts upon these forces. Similarly, while I can understand the motives for my friend's marriage, I cannot fully understand why these particular motives were the decisive ones.

The accessible layers, however, are permeable within the individual by both the personal and physical layers; thus, it matters that the person I am speaking with is in front of my face as opposed to being several thousand miles away. I can truly learn about an individual through her body because the person flows through her body. Likewise, while we cannot directly access the personal level of another individual, we come to understand that person through patterns in his choices and his descriptions of his own motives.

Stein further claims that the two inaccessible layers offer us access to the realms beyond the individual. Through our bodies we interact with the physical world, and the personal layer accesses the realm of value. For example, my body interacts with the fur of my cat, with its texture, color, smoothness, etc. My person recognizes her as a creature that I should be concerned with, that should be treated differently than my books.

This understanding of the individual provides a model that both incorporates causality and motivation and distinguishes the two.

Stein can account for our recognition of both mechanical laws and value. Further, while allowing for empathy that is truly knowledge of the other person's experience, Stein also preserves a personal layer and its personal core that is uniquely private and inaccessible to others, thus preserving a strong sense of freedom and personal responsibility. We can know of the experiences of others, yet not lose our own personhood in that knowledge, and our knowledge of others can be true while also incomplete.

Throughout her phenomenological essays, Stein utilizes and develops her model of the person, and it provides the schema for responding to a further task. She develops these claims in a work she titled 'Contributions to the Philosophical Foundation of Psychology and the Humanities' ('Beiträge zur philosophischen Begründung der Psychologie und der Geisteswissenschaften'), and underlying these essays is the attempt to distinguish and delimit the tasks of psychology and the humanities. Her desire, as she states on the first page, is 'to secure the groundwork for a definition of psychology and the humanities that will fit the facts'. At the turn of the century, psychology was still in the process of breaking off as a field distinct from philosophy, and it was still a branch of philosophy when Stein studied psychology at the University of Breslau. In the early part of the twentieth century, it still was (and perhaps now still is) an open question about precisely what characterizes psychology and distinguishes it from other areas of study. Stein uses the previous distinctions and analyses to come to the conclusion that psychology is the study of the psyche, that is, the sensate level (and the proper realm of lifepower), whereas the humanities explore the realm of the mental and the meaningful. Psychology and the humanities are certainly related insofar as the two layers affect each other. But they are also distinct. Analysis of the objects of study in the humanities requires 'neither natural-science knowledge of the materials that they're founded on, nor any knowledge of psychological processes that had some role to play in the origin of a work' (*PPH*ii, p. 299). Because the mental level is distinct from the physical or sentient, one can come to understand Plato's claims in the *Meno* without knowing about the paper on which the dialogue was written or the psychological state of the author or characters.

Further, Stein claims that psychology is a science because the sensate realm deals with a kind of causal mechanism. But psychology can never be an exact science, in contrast to the physical sciences, because the realm of the sensate is both influenced by the mental (in the transference of meaning into lifepower) and influences the mental in ways that cannot be quantifiably measured. (Even if the previous conditions were not problematic, psychology would also need to have access to the full history of the individual's experiences and the output and intake of lifepower in order to determine the exact state of the psyche. Such a project is highly unlikely and certainly could not be universally determined, as the lifepower capacities differ for different individuals.) Thus, while predictions can be made about the sensate realm and a kind of scientific analysis can be conducted, the exactitude of the physical sciences is neither possible nor desirable in psychology.

Stein concludes that a more appropriate understanding of our experience of others, of human freedom, of our personal structure, and of psychology as a discipline can all be achieved through a more careful study of the phenomena. And Stein attempts to do so in her early phenomenological works, which she nonetheless saw as merely beginning the work that needed to be done.

Notes

1 I recommend the following introductory texts on phenomenology: Herbert Spiegelberg's *The Phenomenological Movement: A Historical Introduction* (The Hague: Martinus Nijhoff, 1971), esp. pp. 653–701; Robert Sokolowski's *Introduction to Phenomenology* (New York and Cambridge: Cambridge University Press, 2000); and I. M. Bocheński's 'Philosophy of Essence' in *Contemporary European Philosophy*, trans. Donald Nicholl and Karl Aschenbrenner (Berkeley, CA: University of California Press, 1956).

2 Herbert Spiegelberg, *The Phenomenological Movement*, Vol. 2, p. 659.

3 Stein was certainly concerned that there were Idealistic tendencies in the post-*Logical Investigations* writings. Not all Husserl scholars, however, agree, and debates regarding whether Husserl was or was not an Idealist continue.

4 This question can be developed by considering issues regarding, what Husserl calls, *constitution*. See Sawicki's *Body, Text, and Science: The Literacy of Investigative Practices and the Phenomenology of Edith Stein* (Boston, MA/Dordrecht: Kluwer, 1997) for a more detailed discussion of Husserl's and Stein's positions on this issue.

5 *Welt und Person*, ESW VI, p. 63.

6 Stein continues to employ this understanding of empathy throughout all of her writings. For example, in her 1941 *Ways to Know God*, Stein presents descriptions strikingly akin to those of her early essays.

7 See Sawicki's development of this theme in the Editor's Introduction in *PPH*.

8 One would, however, need to distinguish an inclination born from the idea of a trip and thus motivated by the content versus one born of exhaustion of resources.

8 At times, Stein distinguishes two strata of lifepower: sensory and mental. See, for example, *PPH*i, pp. 79ff.

9 In a few places, Stein backs off from these claims, suggesting that the principle of individual uniqueness is *a posteriori* rather than *a priori*. See, for example, *EeS*, p. 235 and pp. 458–9.

10 Stein distinguishes *feelings* and *moods*. The first, feelings, are directed toward something; for example, my love for my brother. Moods, however, are more vague; I may in general be cheerful without having some particular thing over which I am cheerful (and thus it may be due to an influx of lifepower). What motivate feelings (in contrast to moods) are values.

3

Social and Political Writings

Edith Stein was deeply attached to her own family and had strong ties, which intensified as she grew older, to her Jewish roots; she developed significant, lifelong friendships within the Philosophical Society at Göttingen; when the First World War broke out, Stein quickly volunteered to serve her country, putting her own career on hold; and when she was middle-aged, she chose to live a communal religious life. Although independent and bold, Stein was not a rugged individualist. In a 1930 essay, she says, '[c]ommunity is necessary; without community, without social life and therefore without the formation of individuals into members of a community, the final end of the human being is not attainable.'[1]

What it means to be an individual is, according to Stein, to be in communion with others. There are no isolated individuals. In her dissertation on empathy, Stein argues that our self-understanding is intimately tied to our relations with others, and in 'Sentient Causality,' she claims that there are energy transfers between individuals. Her thoughts on the community, however, come to a fuller articulation in her second and third *Jahrbuch* essays. The second *Jahrbuch* essay is entitled 'Individual and Community' and was written in 1920, a year after the First World War Armistice was negotiated and not long after Stein left her position as Husserl's assistant (although it was not published until 1922). Her third *Jahrbuch* essay, a study of the state, was completed a year later in 1921 and published in 1925. These texts reveal Stein's intense concern for our communal life and were written at a time in postwar Germany when the problems of social and political life were especially acute.

46

The texts also reveal Stein's awareness of a number of dangerous ideas gaining in power in the opening decades of the twentieth century, among them, Bolshevism, Fascism, and the biologically based theories of race adopted by the National Socialists. She uses the example of Bolshevism in 'Individual and Community' in order to illustrate 'inherited' or merely suggested ideas, and in 'An Investigation of the State,' she argues that states are tools of communities and not themselves communities. Further, she argues, on one hand, against Marxist materialism and, on the other, against attempts to deny any role to our material conditions. In her theory of the person, she makes the body a central concern (although also insisting that we are more than our bodies), and, in her political writings, she regularly discusses the significance of the land in forming a people.

Because Stein's political theory grows out of her theory of the person and the community, it must be read in the context of her other phenomenological writings. In analyzing our communal lives, Stein understands political states as differentiated from, although related to, our communities, which develop from both our mental and sensate levels. In the process of developing her theory of the state, Stein criticizes social contract theory and presents analyses of race, culture, and the relation of states to religion. Each of these will be considered in the following discussion.

On community

After studying under Husserl and working for him for nearly a year and a half, Stein composed her own phenomenological studies of the person and community. It is likely that Stein understood her work as continuing Husserl's project from *Ideas I* and *II* of establishing a foundation for all human sciences, including the natural sciences, the social sciences, and the humanities. Phenomenology was to be that foundation. Stein agreed with Husserl that all knowledge claims could be properly grounded only in phenomenology, and her work was intended to articulate, among other things, the connection between the human and the natural sciences. Thus, her first essay focused largely on the structure of the person and the way in which individuals grasp and understand the world, distinguishing our comprehension of causal and motivational connections. The second *Jahrbuch* essay, 'Individual and Community,' develops these themes on the level of the community, and Stein employs her theory of the person in order to answer the question of how and on what bases community is possible.[2]

Before answering this question, however, Stein distinguishes genuine community from a number of other kinds of unions among people, including *association* and *mass*. The key distinction between *community* (*Gemeinschaft*) and *association* (*Gesellschaft*, also translated as 'society') draws from the work of the German sociologist Ferdinand Tönnies (1855–1936).[3] Tönnies viewed communities as based in organic relations among individuals, whereas associations are based in more artificial unions, for example, voluntary alliances such as a workers' union with merely instrumental ends. Associations have external goals or purposes, the aims of the initial founding acts; in contrast, communities have an internal goal, the well-being of all members. Finally, associations involve *subject–object* relations, while communities require *subject–subject* relations. In a community, Stein says, one does not confront the other person, 'but rather *lives with him* and is determined by the stirrings of his life, they are forming a *community* with one another' (*PPH*ii, p. 130).

Communities range in size from small families and circles of friends to the community of all spiritual or mental beings. And, unlike associations, communities do not arise from optional acts or choices. Rather, they develop organically. Community

grows up and dies out like a living creature. Also, it doesn't serve any external purpose, like the association, but rather – like an organism – has no other purpose than that immanent to it, the purpose of proper development, of the unfolding of its original predisposition. Just as that predisposition is based in the distinctiveness of the individuals who enter into the community, so are all organs and functionings that build up the community determined the same way. (*PPH*ii, p. 261)

Human beings are, Stein claims, by nature communal beings and thus have an inclination 'to reach out beyond themselves toward a complete unification,' toward an 'overcoming absolute loneliness' (*PPH*ii, p. 285).

Despite the strong distinction made between association and community, few alliances are pure associations or pure communities. Our lives are mixed. In principle, however, pure communities are possible, whereas pure associations are not. All associations are derivative from and presuppose communities. Stein gives the example of a demagogue, a leader who wants to manipulate people in order to fulfill his own ends. Such a group is an association ordered for the ends envisioned by the leader and not necessarily shared by the other members. In order to manipulate the crowds, however, the demagogue must understand the motivations of the people, and to that degree, he must – at some point – have been open to others as subjects. Furthermore, he must appeal to them *as subjects* even as he uses them. Therefore, only because he understands community and can appeal to communal relationships can the associative ends be achieved. Similarly, we could think of certain commercials, for example, an advertisement picturing various beautiful, love-filled family scenes. The aim is to sell a product, but it does so by appealing to us as subjects, and the commercial achieves its profit-oriented ends only through an appeal to communal ends and relationships.

The core of Stein's essay is dedicated to a careful articulation of the essential nature of community and its basis in our nature as persons. In order to do so, she makes a number of key distinctions. First, a truly communal union is different from merely having the same reaction to some one stimuli or mere reciprocity based on purely physical or physiological networks. Fifty people responding in the same way to a TV program would not count as a community, nor is a packed train a community. These only become so when there is an openness to the other people, a seeing of the others as subjects and an experience of some event as a collective or communal experience. At the beginning of the essay, Stein gives the example of an army unit that has lost its leader. The leader's death is not one individual's loss but a communal loss. When each looks away from how such a loss affects him or her personally (perhaps the leader was also a close friend) and considers only what it means for the community, then one feels *in the name* of the community. It is not merely that each of us is, in fact, experiencing the same thing; each of us is also aware of it as shared.[4] I do not understand my experience as the same as yours but, rather, I understand the experience as *ours*. Further, with this notion of communal experiences, we can, Stein claims, say whether the community is grieving passionately and deeply, or mildly and fleetingly, and judge whether the community feels the grief appropriately.

Communal experiences are not merely the sum of several individuals' experiences. Rather, communal experiences arise out of the individual experiences, but as something new, as *our* experience and not merely as my individual experience plus your individual experience. Because of this, the things that develop community must be shareable and held in common. Such communal experiences are not identical with empathizing with another. Someone might empathize with me in my grief over my grandmother's death, and this experience might unite us as friends; it nevertheless does not count as a *communal* or shared experience *per se*. In contrast, the army unit's collective loss is communal grief in the way that my personal loss cannot be.

Ironically enough, it is possible to have a communal experience that, nonetheless, only one individual undergoes. If, for example, one individual learns of the leader's death prior to the rest of the community, he may still experience that grief as the community's grief, although no other person in the community yet shares it. Likewise, a communal experience may continue beyond the lifespan of any particular individual or set of individuals. The hatred between groups, for example, is one such communal experience that may extend over many generations. Stein writes somewhat poignantly from her home in Breslau, Germany, at the end of the First World War that communal experiences such as 'the suffering of a conquered people' is 'so vast that the lone [human being] stands before it as before something immense and incomprehensible' (*PPH*ii, p. 143).

Communities thus require openness to other subjects and shared experiences. This sharing requires more than *merely* understanding the other. Perhaps a diplomat guesses what her discussion partner is thinking and chooses her own words and actions in an attempt to outmaneuver the other. She is not then building on the *content* of the other's thought, but rather bases her decisions only on the fact 'that the other *is thinking* this' (*PPH*ii, p. 215). In such cases no common thinking can occur. Each is in, and has only, his or her own world. True community requires a sharing of worlds and an 'open and naive commitment.' Community cannot exist, Stein insists, without a common life, shared values, common sources, and the stirrings of similar motives (*PPH*ii, p. 215). In her dissertation on Stein's theory of community, Sr M. Regina van den Berg strikingly notes that there could be no community among the devils in hell since their hatred of each other and themselves prevents the openness and trust necessary for genuine community.[5] Community is based in shared experience and openness to others; Stein also, however, distinguishes two layers in our communal experiences – the neutral and the sensate.

Community at the mental level

As seen in the previous chapter, Stein's theory of the person describes individuals as having four layers or levels through which we access our experience: the physical, sentient, mental, and personal. In presenting her theory of the community, Stein analyzes the degree to which super-individual unities have each of these layers, and she concludes that the second and third (the sentient and mental) levels are, most properly, the basis of communal relations. (Although the first and fourth levels, the physical and personal levels, are not the primary constituents of communal life, they are not unimportant. All four levels permeate each other within the individual, and thus one cannot fully separate the levels, although they are different in essential structure. Furthermore, each individual, insofar as she is living fully and genuinely, lives out of her personal core, and thus the personal level especially is of great significance for community. Stein dedicates a sizeable section of the essay on community to a discussion of the personal core. See *PPH*ii Chapter 2, §3c.) As Stein understands human beings, our sentient and mental layers are by nature communal, and only if we make an intentional decision can they be closed to the influence of others.

Stein supports her claims regarding the communal nature of the sentient and mental levels by offering a number of examples. We could consider, first, our understanding of empirical facts: Stein argues that what it means to be *empirical* is to be accessible to many people. While my particular sensory experiences are not shared (the cones and rods in my eyes are activated in a way that those of a blind man are not when each of us stand before the *Mona Lisa*), the *meaning* of the experiences and my understanding of them as empirical are communal experiences. When I understand my private sensory experience to be caused by something real, I understand it precisely as the sort of experience that another person could have. And when a scientist observes something, she does it not only for herself but also for all others. Scientific experiments, in order to be truly scientific, must be repeatable. Thus, Stein argues that the empirical is, in fact, what we take to be communal and shared.

She makes an analogous claim about value, arguing that values are as public as empirical observation. When we make a judgment about the empirical world, we have sensory experiences that are inaccessible to others. These private experiences are, however, understood to reveal real objects. In a similar way, Stein claims that our affective responses can reveal the real value of things. Our feelings, however, manifest not the world of objects but the world of value.

In all of her major writings, from her dissertation to her final work on St John of the Cross, Stein discusses value and our apprehension

51

of value. In 'Individual and Community,' Stein develops the claims made in the earlier works, emphasizing the structural similarities between our comprehension of the empirical world and the world of value. She does, however, see one major difference between the two experiences: I can truly perceive the greenness of the trees and yet remain unmoved; I cannot, however, truly perceive the beauty of the landscape without being moved by it. Beauty 'insists that I inwardly open myself to it and let my inner self be determined by it. And for as long at [sic] this inner contact is not effected, for as long as I withhold the response which beauty requires, beauty doesn't entirely divulge itself to me' (PPHii, p. 159). Greenness does not require certain responses on the part of the observer; values do.[6] And, thus, she concludes that ultimately, the value of a person 'is fully and completely accessible only to the lover,' that is, to someone who responds fully to his or her value (PPHii, p. 213).

Empirical observations are by nature communal and can become the basis of a community (one can think of a community of researchers, for example); so too can the perception of values. I may value a book, share that perception with another, and it may become a motive for her actions. The perception of the book's value becomes not simply my experience, but our value and part of a common world. (Values also have an important function in the lifepower circuit, as was seen in the previous chapter. The positive values invigorate and enable a person, whereas the negative values debilitate.)

In these examples there is genuine relation among the subjects, an orientation to the experiences as communal ones and a sense or unitary pattern accessible (in principle) to all. Stein argues that all sense, all meaning, is commonly accessible, and communal experiences owe their unity to 'a sense-content accessible to a plurality of subjects' (PPHii, p. 157). We all access the same content and understand it as ours, as communal. With a somewhat paradoxical example, Stein argues that even mythical and imagined objects can be communal. All of us 'mean the same object when we speak of Sleeping Beauty's castle. But if we all entertain the thought of it, then we have just as many intuitive objects as intuiting subjects' (PPHii, p. 150). Each of us has a different private picture, but the meaning of Sleeping Beauty's castle is nonetheless shared.

Stein understands meaning as something objectively real (although not independent of material objects or thinking beings) and shareable. A meaning is not a subjective opinion or 'what something means to me', but rather a structure or pattern that can be held in common and thus discussed – at least in principle. And we distinguish meaningful and meaningless ideas, sense and nonsense, on the basis of whether it is (in principle) shareable or the sort of thing that another could understand. Thus, all meaning, and therefore our mental level, is at its base communal, and through such sharing of meaning we have a common world.

Community at the sensate level

While relationships on the mental level, including shared meanings and values, are necessary in order to have genuine community, there may also be shared experiences and influences on the sensate level (as seen in the previous chapter). At the sensate level, there is a transfer of lifepower between individuals that works something like an electric circuit. Any one individual can, through a free choice, shut herself off from the lifepower network and thus from part of the communal life. As long as she does not do so, however, she will be affected by the lifepower of her community and will feed into, and draw from, the communal lifepower circuit.

Lifepower is not transferred merely through physical proximity; Stein clearly recognizes a wide variety of ways in which lifepower is transferred. For example, the meaning of a poem can be converted into sensate lifepower and provide inspiration and energy for a number of people. Nonetheless, physical proximity is an extremely powerful way in which lifepower is shared. Consider, for example, the difference between knowing that a friend is working studiously in his office on some problem and having that friend in front of you. Knowing that the friend is working may have little effect on my tiredness, but 'if I have him immediately in front of me and "catch wind of" the mental vigor that I only knew about before, I feel myself stirred by it, too' (*PPH*ii, p. 174).

Thus, Stein claims that all of us contribute to and shape others. There are no lone islands. She says:

[t]he presence of another person prevents certain stirrings from coming over me that would just go ahead and run their course if I were left on my own, while other stirrings are induced in me which I wouldn't be capable of at all on my own ... Because a person's conditions have an influence upon the development of her properties, if other persons are inducing conditions in her, then at the same time they must be (deliberately or inadvertently) contributing to the formation of her character too. (*PPH*ii, p. 266)

Because of the significance of the mental and sensate levels, and because those levels are by nature communal, all our actions and attitudes in some way inform the character of others who share our community life.

There exists, Stein claims, a community power reserve that all help build up and all feed off, and the lifepower of the communal power reserve offers to individuals the opportunity to accomplish more than could be done alone. There may, for example, be an artist who has a tremendous amount of talent, skill, and exemplars, but who lacks on his own sufficient lifepower to work creatively. It is only when he is in communion with others and imbedded within a community that he is able to draw sufficient power to utilize his abilities. Such a person would draw heavily from the communal power reserve, but he may also contribute a great deal to that reserve if his works of art are offered back to the community and become sources of lifepower themselves.

We participate in this power reserve in different ways and to different degrees. Some will contribute more, others less. Some will draw more off the power reserve, others less. One's contributions and one's draws upon this reserve are determined by the amount of lifepower that one has and the way in which he or she is living *as* a member of the community (*PPH*ii, p. 203). Further, Stein claims that the survival of each community depends on *carriers* of the communal life, that is, people with a communal consciousness who display and shape the character of the community and contribute lifepower to the communal reserve. The health of a community is dependent upon the number and depth of devotion of the carriers. Roman Ingarden describes Stein as such a carrier of the communal life of the Göttingen Philosophical Society, and Stein describes her mother as the heart of her own family. While each member contributes to the community, the presence or absence of the carriers of the community have a greater impact on the life of the community than the presence or absence of others.

Among the interesting parts of her essay – particularly in light of the Russian Revolution, which began less than a decade before she wrote her essay, and the speed with which National Socialist ideas swept across the German nation two decades after she completed her study – are her descriptions of ideas transferred 'suggestively' (see *PPH*ii, pp. 244ff.). Because there is interaction between the mental and sensate levels, ideas and meanings can be shared both explicitly and transferred in a more suggestive way. Stein describes such suggestive communication as an acceptance of ideas based not upon our own experiences and insights into connections, but rather based on the experiences and evaluations of others. While such transfers can be problematic, we cannot reject all knowledge that is not gained in a first-person way; we must accept some things on the authority of another. She notes that 'if we wanted to shove aside as *groundless* everything that *didn't* rest upon such a foundation, then practically all of our observations and our science would come crashing down. For what we *ourselves* undergo and examine … rests upon what *others* have undergone and examined' (*PPH*ii, p. 247). But there can be more appropriate and less appropriate ways of taking over convictions, and we must also consider our own 'susceptibility' to certain convictions. Stein provides a brief phenomenology of such transfers and provides an implicit warning that it would serve us well to be attentive to the ways in which meanings and ideas are shared.

On the state

Stein's third *Jahrbuch* essay, and final strictly phenomenological piece, presents a very different kind of relation among people. While her essay on the state builds on the analyses of the previous two works, she is interested less in how individuals are open to one another and more in what characterizes the state structure *per se*. The question she asks throughout is: what is essential to any state, be it human, angelic, or demonic?

Stein was born in 1891, twenty years after the unification of Germany and one year after the succession of Kaiser Wilhelm II to the throne and the dismissal of Bismarck as chancellor. Bismarck left a strong mark on European politics and, in large part due to his efforts, Europe was relatively peaceful during Stein's youth. Germany was recognized as a country of great political and economic influence, and the nation was generally thought to be the greatest military and industrial power in the world. The common German citizen was relatively prosperous, although individuals had limited power in the state. Stein reports many discussions with friends about the relative merits of such a conservative policy versus the more liberal and democratic policies (generally, the more popular position among the country's Catholics).

From 1900 onward, however, Europe became engaged in a series of political crises, many of which arose from the failure of Bismarck's alliances in the absence of the man himself. The assassination of the Austrian Archduke Franz Ferdinand on June 28,

1914 marked the beginning of the First World War, and thus, in the middle of Stein's college years, the relative peace of her childhood was broken and the stability of Germany destroyed. During the years immediately following the war, in addition to defeat and the humiliation of the Versailles Treaty, Germany saw a revolution, the abdication of the emperor, and a new republic. The people were tired, demoralized, and hungry. Inflation was quickly running out of control, and housing was scarce. It was in this climate that Stein wrote her study of the state, setting out to study not the structure of particular states, nor the most appropriate way to feed the war-weary nation, but rather the essential structure of the state *qua state*.

In her early writings, Stein is first and foremost a phenomenologist. She is interested, not in the history of statehood, nor in descriptions of various actual political arrangements, but rather in a description of that which is essential to any state, be it real or imaginary. Her essay includes insightful discussions of the merits and dangers of various political structures (for example, she notes that democracy has the broadest base and marks the clearest example of the idea of the state, but its distortion, ochlocracy, presents 'the greatest imaginable atomization of the state community' ['Eine Untersuchung über den Staat' (UüS), p. 22]). And she presents investigations into civil rights, economy, and revolution. But she always makes clear which elements belong to the state *qua state* and which become significant for certain factually existing states. It might seem unusual, given the political climate of her day, to put so much energy into such an abstract topic. Throughout the essay, however, one sees Stein's conviction that a proper understanding of what is essential to any state – be it a republic, democracy, monarchy, or oligarchy – is not tangential but is in fact crucial for being able to answer more 'practical' questions well. Late in 'An Investigation of the State', Stein provides a number of examples of how misguided theoretical claims have led to badly formed political organizations, and with her questions and concerns, she argues that days of great political upheaval and change may be the time when clarity regarding foundations is most critical.

Stein opens her essay on the state with a discussion of various forms of social organization (mass, community, and association), making clear how states differ from each of these. The key distinction she makes is between *communities* and *states*. States are not communities; they are, however, related to communities (although not in any necessary way). When states develop in an organic way, they are tools of communities, developed for the sake of certain values. For example, a state is often quite useful when a community's membership becomes large or when there is a strong sense of cultural identity which can be better preserved under the structure offered by a state. Stein acknowledges that genuine states are created in more artificial ways. One could think, for example, of a state created by diplomatic decree or one created by a group of devils. Such states are, however, quite vulnerable and easily collapse once the external pressures are removed.[7]

What characterizes both the more artificial and organic states as states, however, is that they have sovereignty. She defines a state as 'a social structure in which free persons are integrated in such a way that one or a majority (in the limit case, all) rule over the others in the name of the whole structure' (UüS, p. 65). Such 'ruling over' requires that the state have the freedom and power to form itself and that it be under the control and forming power of no other organization. The state's sovereignty need not be explicitly formed or stated, but where sovereign power is exercised and – implicitly or explicitly – recognized, one has a state. And none other than states have such sovereignty. Stein clarifies this claim by pointing out that other groups 'could well have the freedom to form themselves (for example, the Church), but they would not be disturbed in their specific character if this freedom were removed from them (for example [the freedom] of the Church by the state)' (UüS 10). Sovereignty belongs essentially to a state, and any group not destroyed by the loss of sovereignty would not be primarily a state.

Sovereignty requires the recognition or consent of the members of the state, although Stein acknowledges that this recognition may be compelled by the state. We could describe a state as a sovereign entity that originates its own organization and power and maintains autonomy. A state may limit its power and accept international laws or other legislative decrees, but it must be a self-limitation on the part of the state, or it ceases to be a state. Where there is sovereignty, there is a state. And if the organization is not sovereign, it is not a state.

As seen above, Stein's understanding of interpersonal relations and organizations is tied to her understanding of the person. As community ultimately depends on, and is derived from, our mental and sentient levels, so statehood depends on, and is derived from, the personal level, our freedom. Because persons are free and self-forming, we can create states endowed with autonomy and forming power. And like persons, states perform spontaneous acts originating in themselves and govern themselves. If the state were subject to another, it would no longer be sovereign and thus no longer a state. Stein makes a number of very strong statements about the extent of our freedom, insisting that, while we can be strongly *motivated* to act in certain ways by the threatening gestures of someone else or the dreadful conditions we face, our true freedom cannot be touched by another. We always maintain our freedom, even under the worst of external circumstances. In an analogous way, a state is defined by its sovereignty, which is maintained even under the strongest of external and internal pressures. If that sovereignty is ever lost, so too is statehood.

Given Stein's emphasis on sovereignty, one may rightly ask how states should be related to other states. Following the debates regarding the League of Nations, Stein wrote that a law of nations would be consistent with the existence of numerous states only if an international body agreed upon a set of resolutions that each member-state enacted in its own territory. Therefore, violation of the law would be violation of *its own* law. Any one of the states could withdraw from the agreement without breaking any laws (although it may be unwise or immoral to do so) because the international group may only make resolutions, not laws with power over the states. The group of nations may decide in common how to legislate themselves, but all legislation ultimately remains self-legislation.

Evaluation of social contract theory

Throughout the essay Stein discusses the quite popular view of the state as arising out of a social contract. John Locke, Thomas Hobbes (1588–1679), and the social contract theorists claim that the state originates in a decision made by a number of individuals who cede their natural rights, bringing the state into being, and that the continuance of the state depends on the consent of those governed. Like the social contract theorists, Stein emphasizes the centrality of freedom, noting that the sovereignty of the state requires the consent of the members (although the state may coerce that consent). And in focusing on consent and such a deliberate and willed choice, a state is thus an association rather than a community (where less rational elements such as lifepower play an important role).

Nonetheless, many of Stein's comments are critical of social contract theory. She argues that while Locke and Hobbes have important insights, they present too simplistic a picture. Contra the social contract theory, states need not (and most frequently do not) arise through a particular, historical act of will, and in emphasizing such acts, social contract theory divides the state too sharply from the communities out of which it arises. In Stein's view, the state is analogous to the personal layer of an individual, and communities are representative of the mental and sensate levels. Just as an individual's freedom is directed and informed by the other layers of the person, so too is the state analogously dependent upon other social organizations.

In most cases, states arise through the creation of an association by a pre-existing community, and the state is thus grounded in, but distinct from, the community (or communities). The state comes into being by formalizing and sanctioning existing communal relations, sometimes adding further structures but building upon the practices already present in the community. And as with persons and communities, actual states grow organically. Consider, for example, a situation where one person is generally looked to for leadership. Out of such a consistent habit may grow a monarchy. The political structure could not come into being, however, without the previous custom of turning to one person for guidance in all situations requiring a certain kind of leadership.

It is possible that the state creates laws which conflict with the customs of the people. Insofar as this occurs, the state will lack a certain inner unity and – to the degree that there is conflict – will be able to maintain its unity only through coercion. Thus, Stein concludes – agreeing with Aristotle (384–322 BC) – that it is first *philia*, friendship or concord, that binds a state together rather than justice (UüS, p. 12). A state is most secure when, first, it is built upon a previously existing community; secondly, the laws that it passes coincide with community relations; and thirdly, the authority of the state is accepted and taken for granted. If the state passes laws that lead the citizens to have misgivings or question the solidity of the state, the state endangers itself and the recognition of its sovereignty necessary for its existence.

Because of her emphasis on community and the organic development of states, Stein sees the origin of the state as a complex affair. It is not produced simply through passing laws (except in the cases of artificial states), but rather is tied to the development of the community. The social institutions develop objectivities, that is, morals, customs, and rights that arise from the ways in which people live. Therefore, the state, although distinct from the community, is strongly related to community.

In a second critique of the contract theory, Stein denies the claim that individuals have 'natural rights' which are ceded to the state.[8] Rather, she says that there are only pure laws and positive laws. (In denying such 'natural rights' or 'natural law,' Stein is not denying the intrinsic value of each individual. But she does think that the social contract theorists have misunderstood what that value consists of.) Drawing heavily on the work of her friend Adolf Reinach, Stein insists that the heart of sovereignty is law, and that the task or calling of a state is to legislate. She then distinguishes two understandings of law: *pure law* and *positive law*. The first holds for all everywhere and is independent of anyone's recognition of the law. Two examples of such a pure law are that a promise ceases to bind someone once it is fulfilled and that one is obligated to repay a debt. In both cases, the very notions – promises and debts – include the rule. A promise is a commitment, and one is no longer committed when one has fulfilled the commitment. Likewise, with the second case, the idea of debt includes the notion of paying back. If one does not intend to pay back what is borrowed, one has not borrowed (and therefore is not in debt), but was rather given something. Thus, pure law is a law that appeals to essential structures. (Stein's view of pure law has similarities with the natural law tradition, and she claims in this essay that 'natural law' is an unclear version of pure law [UüS, p. 54, see also UüS, p. 47].) In contrast, positive law requires law-makers and those bound by the law, and particular positive laws come into being and cease. They vary among different states and peoples, and the making, proclaiming, interpreting, and enforcing of such laws are the key tasks of a state. (The state may take on other tasks, for example, providing regulations or opportunities for trade, education, finance, exploration, etc., but the core of the state lies in its ability to legislate.) Stein recognizes that the state may have other elements that are not strictly necessary for its existence, and she explores a number of such elements, including race, culture, and people.

Race, culture and people

Stein includes in her discussion of the state elements that although important for the development of a state are not essential to a state *qua state*. Among them are a theory of race and discussions of land and economy. None of these are part of the essence of a state; were there a state made up of pure spirits, neither land nor economy nor race would be of importance. But these concerns have a significant place in states as we experience and develop them.

Because we as human beings have bodies and are in need of food and other material resources, our states cannot be without land. But territorial boundaries function in different ways in different states.

Nomadic tribes do not need rigid and stable state lines, although they do need sovereignty over the areas they inhabit. Furthermore, a single state need not exist on the same land throughout its history. Land or territory is not identical with a state, although the particular land inhabited provides an important component for how the state is established and is, in some form or another, a necessary element of all human states.

Stein also sees a further significance for the land. At numerous points throughout both 'Individual and Community' and her essay on the state, Stein describes the influence of the land on the character of the people, and she makes land central to her race theory. Stein does not understand *race* to be, as the National Socialists claimed, based in our biology. Rather, according to Stein: 'racial traits simply exhibit the ingenuity of human persons who find unique ways to live in various sorts of places on earth. For example, the desert breeds mystical poets, the mountains produce self-reliant adventurers. Race arises through creative adaptations of this kind.'[9] The land helps shape the character of a race. It does not do so *causally*, but *motivationally*. (As seen in the previous chapter, Stein carefully distinguishes motivations and causes.) The characteristics of a particular race do not lie in someone's 'blood' or biological features, nor are they in any way causally efficacious. (Stein argues that race does not determine destiny, as Alfred Rosenberg and other Nazi theorists later argued.) Rather, she claims that because of a group of individuals' geographical situation, there are motivations to develop certain traits, temperaments, and sensibilities. Thus, Stein understands race and type as arising out of our living together with certain influences, conditions, and shared objectives.

Stein distinguishes *race* from *community*. Community requires communication, that is, a 'we' orientation and openness to the group. Race has no such interpersonal element. Once the move to a group consciousness is made, one may have not merely a race, but a *folk* or *people* [*Volk*]. Like a race, a people has a stamp of being of a certain type, but they are further united through a shared culture (although the culture may be either bigger or smaller than the people).

Stein dedicates a considerable part of the essay to making careful distinctions among various kinds of groups, distinguishing *race* from a *people*, and a *people* from a *tribe* and *nation*. Among the most interesting is her characterization of a *people*. She says:

> a community of the breadth and scope of a people [*Volk*] is to be taken as a *folk* community [*Volksgemeinschaft*], then, only when

and so long as its own *culture*, determined by its specific character, emerges from its spirit. Every culture, that is, every unified and delimited cosmos of spiritual goods ... points back to a spiritual center to which it owes its origin, and this center is a creative community whose specific psychic character affects and is reflected in all its productions. (UüS, p. 14)

The words used here for 'spirit' and 'spiritual,' '*Geist*' and '*geistig*,' are common German words and can also be translated as 'mind' and 'mental' or 'intellectual.' In the claim above, Stein insists that what is distinctive about a culture is, first, that it has a unified character and, second, that it responds creatively to all areas of value, presenting a 'cosmos of spiritual goods,' all of which reflect its spirit or character.

In 'An Investigation of the State,' Stein describes history as 'the realization of values' and culture as a comprehensive response to all value areas (UüS, p. 117). Frequently, individuals respond to some values and not to others; someone may respond to aesthetic values, developing his dispositions in this area while failing to fully appreciate scientific values. Part of what characterizes the uniqueness of individuals is the particular values to which they respond. In contrast, a culture requires a response to *all* values. There can be certain emphases in a particular culture, but no area of value can be fully lost. Therefore, interestingly enough, what is essential to a *people*, as a community with a culture, is an openness to a wide variety of individuals, ensuring a receptivity to all areas of value. All partial emphases must complement one another in order to achieve a full response to the world of value. What distinguishes one culture from another is the distinctive way in which each responds to the world of value. In a short footnote, Stein speaks positively about Spengler's influential book *The Decline of the West*, describing his great achievement as the right emphasis on the symbolic character of cultural artifacts and their relation to the soul or character of a people (UüS, p. 14). Creative cultural power is, according to Stein, the *sine qua non* of a people.

Lengthy discussions of culture and peoples are not, Stein claims, out of place in a study of the state. While not essential for a state, the people or folk communities are nonetheless important. Stein even goes so far as to say that a state *needs* a people – not in order to be a state, but in order for actual states to thrive. The creative power of a people provides direction and legitimation for a state, and without such a foundation the state is brittle and hollow, lacking an 'inner warrant for its existence' (UüS, p. 15). Stein is deeply critical of states that are not based in a people or peoples. For example, she describes Frederick the Great's Prussian state as 'eerie,' without life or soul (UüS, p. 23). It is the community and culture that feed and nourish individuals, and commitment to a state not grounded in a community or group of communities is like commitment to a machine.[10] Stein understands the role of the state as offering protection so that communities and culture, which nourish the individual, may develop and flourish. The state may also help integrate and unite a culture that has become so large that few individuals see the whole and the relations among the parts. Thus, there is a reciprocal relation: a people may give rise to a state when and if it needs the protection of a state in order to preserve its culture, and the state needs a people in order to provide its legitimacy as well as direction, energy, and creativity.

Stein concludes that sharp separations of social and political history are misguided. The fate of a state is not separate from the intellectual, moral, aesthetic, and religious achievements of the people, nor, incidentally, can the story of the culture be separated from its political accomplishments. (The latter may, however, play the more important role in the study of history because they reflect more stable historical structures.) But, not surprisingly, Stein in her analysis of race, culture, and people does not distinguish the roles of morality and religion in relation to the state.

The state and religion

Stein distinguishes the state and various community relations, claiming that they are related but distinct in their essential structure. Because of this, Stein denies that serving 'a kingdom of morals' is a task belonging properly to the state. She makes the strong claim that '[t]he moral cannot be legislated' (UüS, p. 109). The moral (in contrast to the lawful) has to do with value and orientation to value, and value is grasped through feelings. Individuals can respond to values; a state, however, cannot. It has neither a soul nor feelings, and it is not moral in the way that individual persons are. Those who wish to make the state a moral kingdom should target, not the state, but the people. (Moreover, the state, in order to retain its legitimacy, must conform to the ethos of the people, and, therefore, one cannot improve the state without improving the base of the state.) Ultimately, Stein claims that the areas of the person making one moral or not are outside of the direct control of the state. (They are not, however, outside of the indirect control. She does claim that because motives are an essential part of the formation of character the state may encourage certain moral stances through its laws [UüS, pp. 76, 109].)

Stein is careful in how she makes her claims. She does not claim that morality should have no part in the state, but rather that morality has a part in the state *because* it has a part in the lives of the people. A theocracy, for example, which in no way separates morals and politics or religion and the state, could be a legitimate state. Because it grows out of a religious community, the laws and directives of a theocracy in their content could well coincide with certain moral and religious claims, although in its form *qua state* a theocracy is no more moral or religious than any other state. Similarly, Stein claims that states do not establish culture or educate their citizens, although they may provide the structures and space for such activities, safeguarding their development.

These claims become more intelligible in the light of her theory of the person and her analogy between the state and the person. Stein distinguishes four layers to the person and the state represents only one of those layers. Like the layers in the person, however, one layer cannot live without the other three and there is interpenetration between the various layers. Thus, we need to distinguish the essential structure of the state *qua state* from the elements necessary for its healthful functioning. As a state *qua state*, it does not nourish human souls, but it is in the interest of the state to develop space where culture and community can be developed. As a kind of association, the state is defined only by the free actions of its representatives. But, as in the case of persons, free acts are motivated by rational and sensate concerns. Therefore, properly speaking, customs, motives, morals, and religious impulses have no direct part of the state but do play a role indirectly because of the state's dependence on communities.

Stein dedicates the final section of her essay to a discussion of the relationship between the state and religion, raising the question of whether there is an inevitable conflict between the two. The religious sphere claims priority over all others, and we are to obey God's commandments unconditionally. Such a situation seems to be incompatible with the sovereignty claimed by the state, and there appear to be two mutually exclusive claims on our obedience. Given the situation, it is little surprise that conflicts arise (as occurred during Bismarck's *culture wars* that led to the founding of the

German monastery at Echt, in the Netherlands, where Stein lived during her last years).

There is no solution, at least not in principle, to this conflict (UüS, p. 118). There are only various compromises (one of which is a theocracy). Stein quotes Jesus's command to 'give unto Caesar what is Caesar's' as giving us permission to recognize state sovereignty, and if the state *of its own accord* incorporates His second command to give unto God what is God's, there will be no actual conflicts between our religious and political allegiances. Further, Stein points out that, on a principle of prudence, it is in the state's own interest not to endanger its legitimacy by creating laws that violate the consciences of its citizens. There may also be other compromises, such as making allowances for conscientious objectors. But ultimately, she says, the conflict cannot be fully resolved, for it is not part of the essence of a state to be either holy or unholy, whereas individuals must become one or the other.

Stein joined the Catholic Church within a few months of finishing her essay on the state, and one can see throughout the piece marks of her growing interest in and conviction of the truth of Christianity. She speaks of the duties of believers in a tone identifying herself among them, directly addresses questions of religion and the state, and has a substantial footnote on the distinction between legal guilt and sin.

In her post-conversion writings, however, Stein does not again address the state in detail, although in a 1936 piece she does footnote her earlier essay with a positive commendation (see *EeS*, p. 380). She does, however, discuss community again in her post-conversion writings, often emphasizing the community of the faithful. For example, she writes in 1930:

> [t]hrough the fall of the first man, ruin came upon the whole race; and as we all fell in Adam, so we are all saved in Christ. No one comes to the Father except through Him, that is, through entrance into the community of the saved, through membership in the mystical Body of Christ. So we have in the mystery of salvation a valid witness that *community* is necessary *in order to attain salvation*.[11]

There is some debate among the scholars about how many of the details of her early phenomenological work on the person and community are retained in her later texts. Marianne Sawicki has claimed that very little is retained;[12] in contrast, Sr M. Regina van den Berg argues the opposite, claiming that in fact Stein has retained most of her understanding both of individuals and communities in her post-conversion works, although developing a number of significant points and employing different philosophical terms.[13] It is clear, however, that Stein's primary interests became more explicitly Christian after 1922, and few of her writings after her baptism fail to include explicit discussions of our relation to God.

Notes

1 'Die theoretische Grundlagen der sozialen Bildungsarbeit' in *ESGA* 16, p. 16.

2 Sawicki provides an excellent discussion of the relationship between Stein's writings and Husserl's and Scheler's, in 'Husserl and Stein on the State: Toward a Critique of Race Theory' at *www.jewel.morgan.edu/~sawicki/ esstaat.html*, as well as *Body, Text and Science*.

3 Tönnies's most famous work is *Gemeinschaft und Gesellschaft*, trans. Charles P. Loomis as *Community and Society* (East Lansing, MI: Michigan State University Press, 1957).

4 If there is no awareness of an event as shared, although mutual influence upon each other, then the group in question would be a *mass* rather than a community. See *PPH*ii, p. 241 and UüS, p. 1.

5 M. Regina van den Berg, 'Community in the Thought of Edith Stein' (PhD dissertation, Catholic University of America, Washington, DC, 2000), p. 125.

6 In a brief and fascinating section, Stein distinguishes genuine and 'sham sentiments,' or emotional attitudes that 'awaken without any *axiological* basis' (*PPH*ii, p. 253). See also *PPH*ii, pp. 267ff. Sham emotions may influence us and become formative, yet they nonetheless retain a certain hollowness because they do not arise from a full perception of a value. In contrast, all genuine emotions are responses to perceptions of value.

7 Stein does grant the possibility that such an artificial state may lead to the development of a community.

8 In UüS I, §2f, Stein does endorse a notion of subjective right, understanding a subjective right as a capacity with a corresponding duty.

9 Marianne Sawicki, 'Husserl and Stein on the State,' p. 14. See also UüS, pp. 86ff.

10 Stein concludes her comments on this point by saying:

> it appears to us much more natural and intelligible when someone loves his folk and only derivatively the state as its external form, than when the state is loved immedi-

ately for itself. The final remarks are not meant to deny that a state *not* resting on the foundation of a folk could not also have from the standpoint of the community a great value: it could secure the free development of persons and communities living under its care (UüS, pp. 23–4).

11 Stein, 'Die theoretischen Grundlagen der sozialen Bildungsarbeit', in *ESGA* 16, pp. 17–18.

12 See, for example, Sawicki's 'Edith Stein's *Philosophy of Psychology and the Humanities*: The *Jahrbuch* Treatises of 1922,' presented at Dusquesne University on March 11, 2000.

13 See her dissertation, 'Community in the Thought of Edith Stein', esp. Chapter 5.

4

Woman and Women's Education

Between 1928 and 1932, under the organizing power of Fr Erich Przywara, Stein gave a series of lectures and radio addresses in Germany, Switzerland, and Austria, speaking as often as fifteen times in as many locations over the course of twenty days.[1] Her letters from those years reveal her exhaustion; she says that her task as a lecturer hit her 'like an avalanche' (*Letters* no. 89). When the competing mounds of grading and travel became too much in 1931, she left her teaching position at Speyer in order to write and speak full-time. She also entertained hopes that she could obtain a university position. Although that dream eluded her, many of her talks were published in various journals and periodicals, and she gained a reputation as a spokesperson for the Catholic Women's Movement and leader of teaching reform.

Among her central concerns in these lectures are clearly questions of whether there is a feminine nature and how we should understand the education and vocation of women. Stein consistently affirms her commitment to a distinctive feminine nature, but she also insists on genuine equality between the sexes and emancipation in all professional spheres. There are thus three main foci: first, the distinctiveness of the feminine (and masculine) nature; secondly, the implications of such a nature for feminine vocations; and, finally, a model for women's education.

Feminine nature

As far as is known, Stein's first public lecture was given on April 12, 1928 in Ludwigshafen, Germany, to a group of Catholic teachers. Her topic was 'The Significance of Woman's Intrinsic Value in National Life,' and she begins by describing the progress of the feminist movement. In turn-of-the-century Germany, women were seen by the law as minors and placed in the same class as children and the mentally retarded. The feminist movement (in which Stein, during her student days, was active as a member of the Prussian Association for Women's Suffrage) was then concerned primarily with emancipation, that is, with the 'removal of the fetters which prevented women from entering into the same educational and professional activities *as men*' (*Essays on Women* [*EW*], p. 254).

Critics of such emancipation and the women's movement, however, insisted that 'a woman's place is in the home,' and they feared that such emancipation would jeopardize women's calling as mothers. The critics (and dominant popular opinion) insisted that women were not capable, or were less capable, of working in certain 'masculine' professions. The feminist movement often responded to its critics by denying any female nature or singularity, and because of this, as Stein describes the situation, 'one could not speak of an intrinsic *feminine value*' (*EW*, p. 254). The early battles of the feminist movement thus drew a line between those in support of the emancipation of women, who denied an essential female nature, and those against female emancipation, who affirmed such a nature. No ground remained for the support of both emancipation and gender differences.

With the 1919 changes in the Weimar Constitution, however, much of the initial battle in Germany was ended. The law insisted on genuine equality and an equal standing before the law, and thus women became full citizens. With this victory for those supporting emancipation, the country was now ready, Stein claims, to raise the question of whether women have either a distinctive nature or a distinctive value as women. Stein herself answers both questions with a yes. She clearly affirms real equality and emancipation, yet she also claims that there are real differences between the two equal sexes. Thus, in her lectures, she argues for the claim that there is a real feminine distinctiveness without thereby undermining the equality of the sexes.

Stein sees her own work on the nature of women as preliminary; she had at her disposal few psychological studies on the topic, and, as she points out, there needs to be 'serious, scientific treatment' of the uniqueness of women (*EW*, p. 164). Furthermore, as Lucy Gelber, the original editor of Stein's texts, notes, 'there were no preliminary works whatever written from a religious point of view on which she could base her findings' (*EW*, p. 15). Stein's work on the distinctiveness of the feminine psyche broke ground that had been little touched.

Before, however, she makes claims as to where that distinctiveness lies, she affirms her commitments both to a common human nature and to the uniqueness of each individual. She says, 'no woman is only *woman*' (*EW*, p. 49). Each woman, just as each man, has her own individual talents and capacities, be they artistic, scientific, technical, intellectual, or otherwise. No one has merely, or purely, a feminine or masculine nature. Stein is strongly critical of any essentialism that attempts to deny the uniqueness of each person. Rather, each of us is human, and within human nature there is a division between the feminine and the masculine. Individual persons, however, do not fall simply into one category or the other. In general, more females have feminine traits, and they tend toward the feminine, while males tend toward the masculine, but all of us have our distinctive individual nature and may realize the feminine or masculine nature to different degrees and in differing ways. Thus, the nature of any woman is always threefold, including: the common human nature, her wholly individual nature, and that specific to her as a woman.

Stein is wary of positions which undermine either our unique individuality or our common human nature; she is not, however, a historicist. She does not think that all differences between the sexes can be traced simply to historical conditions (although perhaps some can). Stein claims that there is a feminine species that 'cannot be modified by environmental, economic, cultural, or professional factors' (*EW*, p. 174). The task of specifying the distinctiveness of that species, however, is difficult and highly controversial. Stein's own position is arrived at, she says, through philosophical and phenomenological study and through an interpretation of the Old and New Testaments. Her own studies in psychology, years of teaching experience, and observation clearly play a role, but her primary method of analysis appears to be phenomenological (although she gives us less of the process she uses to reach her conclusions in her lectures on women than she did in her writings for Husserl's *Jahrbuch*). As in all her phenomenological work, she expects us to test her claims against our own experience and understanding.[2] Stein also has parallel arguments for her claims that draw from revelation, and she repeatedly appeals to Scripture in explicating her position. Her basic claims do not depend on revelation, but in her development of the insights one can see her deeply religious worldview and her attempt to develop a fully Christian anthropology.

Stein points to two distinctive characteristics of the feminine. First, she claims that women have an orientation toward the personal, whereas men are more objective, and secondly, she claims that women are directed toward the whole, whereas men tend to compartmentalize. She says of man, 'it is natural for him to dedicate his faculties to a discipline (be it mathematics or technology, a trade or business management) and thereby to subject himself to the precepts of this *discipline*' (*EW*, p. 255). In contrast, woman is oriented toward people and the personal; her concern is for living things, especially her own personal life and that of others. She focuses on the living, concrete person and involves her total being in her work, not dividing the various aspects of her life. Whereas men tend to have a one-sided development because of their submission to some discipline, women have a drive toward totality and full development, both of themselves and others.

In saying that women are more personally and less objectively oriented, Stein is not claiming that women are less capable of abstract thought; rather, as Mary Catharine Baseheart puts it, 'characteristically women are not content to remain on the level of the abstract.'[3] There is a drive in the feminine to relate the conceptual back to the concrete, the psychological back to particular psyches, and the theoretical back to the world of experience. Thus, the orientation toward the personal and the concrete need not be a denial of the abstract and conceptual, but it does indicate a dissatisfaction with the merely abstract and conceptual, and an unhappiness with only a part when one can be oriented to the whole.

Alternatively, Stein distinguishes the distinctiveness of men and women by pointing to the threefold human task (taken from the first chapters of Genesis): to know the world, to enjoy the world, and to form it creatively. While all three are human tasks, the feminine is oriented primarily toward the second, that of enjoying and cherishing creation. Such enjoyment requires emotional sensitivity and an orientation toward all living things. Therefore, the strengths of women include a concern for concrete things and emotional responsiveness to their value. Whereas the masculine is characterized by 'bodily strength, the ability for predominantly abstract

71

thought, and independent creativity,' the feminine is characterized by 'feeling, intuition, empathy, and adaptability' (*EW*, p. 82). Women are made to love and cherish all living things and to desire their full development. The feminine, thus, is characterized by a responsiveness to the real.

While Stein employs language suggesting a division between the feminine and the masculine, it is a mistake to think of feminine and masculine distinctivenesses in terms of exclusive traits. The traits in question are primarily human ones, and all powers that are present in masculine nature are also present in feminine nature. In a discussion following one of the lectures, Stein clearly states that being human is fundamental, being a woman is secondary.[4] Nonetheless, one can talk about a feminine or masculine nature because the human traits 'may generally appear in different degrees and relationships' (*EW*, p. 80). Thus, when Stein makes claims regarding the distinctiveness of the sexes, she does not mean to imply that the traits discussed are in any way exclusive. She does think, however, that there is, in general, a relative priority among certain traits and tasks that distinguishes the feminine and masculine.

Because of our individual differences, and therefore the illegitimacy of ascribing to all women certain blanket 'feminine' traits and to all men 'masculine' traits, Stein insists that there should be no legal barriers regarding occupations. There can be no professions solely for women, with others reserved solely for men (*EW*, p. 81). Moreover, she argues that, ultimately, each of us should embody the ideals of both the feminine and the masculine nature:

> The further the individual continues on this path, the more Christlike he will become. Christ embodies the ideal of human perfection: in Him all bias and defects are removed, and the masculine and feminine virtues are united and their weaknesses redeemed; therefore, His true followers will be progressively exalted over their natural limitations. That is why we see in holy men a womanly tenderness and a truly maternal solicitude for the souls entrusted to them while in holy women there is manly boldness, proficiency, and determination. [*EW*, p. 84]

Thus, while Stein affirms differences between the sexes and is willing to describe what those differences involve, she enjoins caution about all claims regarding sexual differentiation. Such differences are so mitigated by our individual uniqueness and our common humanity that neither legal restrictions which oversimplify the differences, nor religious ideals which are blind to a life of full human virtue are appropriate.

Stein repeatedly argues that women can authentically practice any profession. There is, however, a feminine *way* of doing each task, or a way of bringing the feminine singularity to any task. For example, in medicine, even in its specialized fields, 'it should not be forgotten that in most cases it is not only the organ but, on the contrary, it is the entire person who is sick along with the organ' (*EW*, p. 262). A particularly feminine practice of medicine would require an attunement to the whole person and a concern for the patient's whole well-being, even if only one organ is under direct examination. Likewise, in scholarship, which may at first appear as an austere discipline, a feminine orientation will turn the research in personal directions. There may be professions in which one's feminine distinctiveness is easily appreciated and for which there is a sympathetic rapport: for example, nursing, education, and social work. In each of these, the personal attitude and a concern for the development of persons are central. Nonetheless, all professions can be practiced in an authentically feminine way insofar as they are concerned with concrete human life. Even the most abstract of research is connected back to the needs and development of living things, and insofar as one works with others in a laboratory, factory, or office, there is 'an immediate opportunity ... for development of all feminine virtues' (*EW*, p. 50). Wherever there are people and living beings, 'she will find opportunity to sustain, to counsel, to help' (*EW*, p. 264). In fact, the feminine virtues may be especially needed in those places where there is a danger of overspecialization or mechanization, leading to the loss of humanity. Not only are women capable of practicing any vocation or profession, it is also desirable to have women working in all the diverse vocations and professions.

The feminine singularity provides an appropriate and right orientation toward the world,[5] which may be fruitful in any area of work. Stein is not, however, unambiguously enthusiastic. One cannot simplistically paint feminine nature as a shining ideal that offers a cure for all of society's ills. Feminine nature should be seen as neither demonic nor angelic. It is, like all human potential, valuable and beautiful, but also in need of development, and it may be developed rightly or corrupted.

Stein gives several examples of deformed versions of the personal attitude, pointing to, for example, an inappropriate concern for persons that leads to a blind, unrealistic attitude about oneself and others. In such a case, the woman loses the ability to endure criticism, which is seen as an attack upon her person. Her own children are the best, her husband the best, and so on. Or someone may have an overly intrusive interest in the lives of others, a busyness resulting in 'a perverse desire to penetrate into personal lives' (*EW*, p. 257). Rather than waiting for the other to reveal him or herself, she may push to know, understand, and invade the interior life of the other. Likewise, the interest in the personal may result in a desire to lose oneself completely in another person, a desire to sacrifice everything for the sake of another, which ends in an excessive passivity doing justice neither to her own humanity nor that of others. Every need of the other becomes her law and every concern of another is her own. She loses herself (and thereby her own ability to help others develop themselves) in her interest in the other, and in her concern for persons, she fails to be herself a full person.

A different kind of degeneration may result from a malformed desire for totality and orientation to the whole; one may end in a kind of superficiality that skims the surface of everything but plunges deeply into nothing. Her life ends up filled with things and trinkets in an effort to miss nothing, but lacks depth and therefore real development. Or the concern for the concrete and orientation toward the needs of living things may end in greed and an 'anxious, avaricious scraping together and hoarding of things for which she has no use,' a life dedicated to primitive needs and mere sensuality (*EW*, p. 74).

Whereas the degeneration of the masculine nature leads to a 'brutal despotism over creatures – especially over woman' and a tendency to allow his work to dominate him to the point of atrophy of his own development, the degeneration of the feminine nature goes in an opposite direction, including a 'servile dependence on man' and a superficiality that is primarily sensual (*EW*, p. 190). The masculine nature, when it is not appropriately developed, tends toward aggression, and the feminine toward passivity. The fallen masculine nature results in a kind of tunnel vision, one-sidedly focusing on his work, whereas the fallen feminine nature lacks the depth needed to correct this, limiting itself merely to the superficial and therefore losing its spiritual center in a sensuous life.

Stein recommends two things as correctives for such degeneration in the feminine nature. First, she suggests that objective work of any variety – housework, a trade, or science – will help develop an appropriate evaluative distance. Anything that requires 'submitting to the laws of the matter concerned' encourages a degree of objectivity in regard to one's moods, emotions, and disposition. A woman's emotional life should not be stifled, but neither should it be blinding. In such focused tasks a kind of freedom from the self may be gained, and there can be a curtailing of excessive interest in the personal as well as a check on the tendency toward superficiality. Thus, Stein insists that all young women should receive some kind of vocational training. (Such training should not, however, lead to the opposite error, that of 'relinquishing of the good and pure personal attitude nor to a one-sided specializing and enslavement to a discipline which typifies the perversion of masculine nature' [EW, p. 48]. Women should not become like men. The goal is not an adoption of the masculine nature, but Stein does encourage a check on possible excesses and thus a genuine development of the feminine nature.)

But in addition to such objective work, Stein insists that divine grace is necessary in order to overcome a malformation of one's nature. The deepest changes cannot come through external education or formation; rather, '[o]nly the power of grace can uproot and form fallen nature anew; it happens from within, never from without' (EW, p. 48). We cannot through books or sheer will-power clip all the 'wild shoots' within ourselves or others. Such full formation requires supernatural aid. But in the turn to divine help, the feminine nature is well-served for, Stein says, 'the *intrinsic value of woman* consists essentially in *exceptional receptivity for God's work in the soul*, and this value comes to unalloyed development if we abandon ourselves confidently and unresistingly to this work' (EW, p. 259).

Several commentators interpret Stein as saying that biological differences between men and women are the source of the differences in orientation, and that masculinity and femininity in the soul result from differing physical make-up, although the differences are not, in the end, simply physical.[6] On this interpretation, the souls of all human beings would be identical, but the differences in our bodies would stamp a woman's or man's soul in distinct ways. I do not find this to be an adequate interpretation. Stein certainly says that women are formed to be mothers and companions, and she sees the whole of a woman, both physical and psychological, as oriented toward motherhood. But she also says that it 'is not *as* absurd as it may appear at first glance' to think that there may be a transition from physically male to female (EW, p. 174). Although Stein considers the physical change of sex as a possibility, she nonetheless insists on masculinity and femininity as two unchanging species. Therefore, it appears that a better interpretation of her position is to see the masculine and feminine natures as residing first in the soul, not the body. Further, in a 1931 letter to colleagues at Speyer, Stein argues that matter serves the form, not vice versa, and thus the psyche and not the body is primary (*Letters*, no. 100). Similarly, throughout *Finite and Eternal Being*, Stein develops the same argument, insisting that form does not serve the matter, but rather matter serves form. Thus, it appears that feminine souls are well-suited to feminine bodies, but the body is not the *reason* that the soul is feminine.

Nonetheless, in a couple of very brief passages Stein makes the provocative suggestion that the relation of soul and body may differ in men and women, suggesting that in women the union may be more intimate. She says, '[w]oman's soul is present and lives more intensely in all parts of the body, and it is inwardly affected by that which happens to the body; whereas, with men, the body has more pronouncedly the character of an instrument which serves them in their work and which is accompanied by a certain detachment' (*EW*, p. 95). Women are present to and affected by their bodily lives in a way that men are not. Again in her Münster lectures, Stein asserts that the relation of body and soul differs for men and women, and this difference is connected to their psychic lives. Clearly, there is, according to Stein, some way in which a woman's body and her reproductive role are related to the union of body and soul, and this intimate union is connected to the entire nature of the woman and thus all that she does.

The vocation of women

Stein describes the great sickness of her own time as 'an inner disunion, a complete deficiency of set convictions and strong principles, an aimless drifting' (*EW*, p. 259). Society, just as so many individuals, lacked a sense of itself and was lost in a kind of internal chaos. In the midst of this chaos and disunity, many people sought an anesthetic in pleasures, looking always for new and more refined pleasures. But such solutions cannot solve the problem or provide a sense of identity; the pursuit of mere pleasures only intensifies the sickness. The only answer to such disunity is whole persons and the full development of our humanity. In this, Stein sees a task for women. Women are oriented toward persons and personal development, and it is only such personal development that will give each of us identity and help us to become healthy, and, consequently, only such personal development can help society to become so. Stein says, 'when women themselves are once again whole persons and when they help others to become so, they create healthy, energetic spores supplying healthy energy to the entire national body' (*EW*, p. 260). Thus, the particularity of the feminine is, she insists, precisely what is needed to address the problems of her own time, and she repeatedly calls women to take up, firmly and lovingly, the task of becoming full persons. It is not, she says, merely a personal task but is precisely what is necessary for the whole society.

The task of becoming a full human being and helping others become so has a supernatural dimension, and in the 'Fundamental Principles of Women's Education,' Stein presents the feminine task in a transcendent light. A woman is to bear the burdens, both those clearly known and those hidden, which each carries; she is to search out and find the weaknesses in others and to encourage the development of the hidden potentialities. In these tasks she develops the image of God in each of us, and '[o]nly the one who stands with wholesome awe before human souls will search in such a manner, one who knows that human souls are the kingdom of God, who knows that one may approach them only if one is *sent* to them' (*EW*, p. 133). Stein sees in the feminine nature a reflection of God's love. As God's love is poured out freely on all in need, 'healing the sick and awakening the dead to life, protecting, cherishing, nourishing, teaching, and forming,' as God rejoices with the joyful and mourns with the sorrowful and calls us to become what He intends us to be, so also are women called to love, heal, protect, cherish, nourish, teach, and form, rejoicing and sorrowing, wanting always for the other to become whole (*EW*, p. 53).

The vocation of women *qua women* and the task fitting to the feminine nature is the development of full human beings, and throughout her lectures, Stein consistently invokes two images for this task: first, that of helpmate and second, that of motherhood. Stein regularly returns to Genesis 2 where God says that it is not good that man be alone, and thus He created a fit helpmate and companion. In both body and soul, a woman is oriented toward others, to be a companion. Whereas man is 'consumed by "his enterprise"' and has difficulty becoming involved in others and their concerns, such an interest is natural for woman, and becoming involved empathetically in the concerns of others, even concerns far from her own, is part of her personal orientation. In this, a woman is a helpmate. She is suited and oriented toward companionship. In a particularly beautiful passage, Stein says of the woman, 'where a human being is alone, especially one in bodily or psychological need, she stands lovingly participating and understanding, advising and helping; she is the companion of life who helps so that "man is not alone".'[7]

Likewise, the orientation toward the personal, the concrete and living, toward the full development of each being, are all fitting for a woman as a mother. She must, in order to work for the development of a child's potential, intuit and feel that which is not yet, but which could be. In order to help another grow, she must sense what he or she is going through, even when the child cannot clearly express it. And she must, above all, love the child, cherishing it and yearning for its wholeness. All these tasks reflect the centrality of emotions and the focus on persons, emphases characteristic of the feminine nature.

Stein claims that images of companion and mother are appropriate to the feminine, but by this, she does *not* mean that all women should be married or be biological mothers. What Stein means by motherhood and companionship are not simply physical motherhood and marital companionship; the tasks of companionship and motherhood can be taken up by any woman, regardless of her actual state in life, and spiritual companionship and spiritual motherhood 'extend to all people with whom woman comes into contact' (*EW*, p. 132). One may act as a spiritual companion and mother whether one is physically so or not, and both those who have children and those who do not have a call to spiritual motherhood. There is always the supernatural calling to help form people to be children of God.

Perhaps unsurprisingly in postwar Europe, Stein returns repeatedly to the question of the single life, and she emphatically states that there is a distinctive and right motherly task for the single woman. In the Old Testament, women effected their salvation by bearing children, and the focus for women was primarily on marriage and maternity. (While there are certainly exceptions to this in Deborah and Esther, they are so noteworthy precisely because they are so exceptional.) With the New Testament, a new ideal is put forward, that of virginity, of a single life called by God.[8] Virginity, according to Stein, is not to be seen as a renunciation of something that is nonetheless the center of one's desire. Rather, it is the positive desire for union with God, to be the Spouse of Christ.

The call to such a life need not have come through a particular voice or conviction; God also calls us to certain tasks through the external circumstances of our lives. One may discover the call to a single life through the failure to marry as much as through a positive inner conviction. Perhaps because of her own experience, or perhaps because of her many years of counseling women, Stein consistently and repeatedly denies that blind fate, rather than God, deals us our life's condition. God's love is with us in all the details of our lives. He does not abandon us to whims of history or chance, but works His will in all the events of our lives. In an oft-quoted line she says, '[w]hat did not lie in *my* plan, did lie in *God's* plan' (*EeS*, pp. 109- -10). She then goes on to say that the conviction has grown ever deeper in her that

> as seen by God – there is no *accident*, that my whole life in all details is traced out in the plan of the divine Providence and before the all-seeing eyes of God is a perfect whole [*Sinnzusammenhang*: context]. Then I begin to rejoice for the light of glory in which this whole will also be unveiled to me. This is valid, moreover, not only for the individual human life but also for that life of all humanity and furthermore for the whole of all beings. (*EeS*, p. 110)

Stein is confident that in all details our lives are ruled by God and that God may use the unfolding events of our lives to call us to His plan.

Despite her regular insistence that what she means by mother-liness is a spiritual motherliness and not merely a biological one, Stein does not deny the great significance of biological motherhood. In a radio address, she says that it is her conviction that there is no natural power so influential to the fate and character of a person as his or her mother. (And our fate, after all, lies in our character.) There is a mysterious connection between a child and her mother. Thus, as biological mothers, women (because of the feminine nature) may be called to carry more than half the load for the care of the family, and, as Stein puts it, the mother is to 'be there' for her child. Stein is quick to insist, however, that this does not mean always *being with* the child. Being a biological mother is not incom-patible with being a professional as well, and Stein strongly states that '[o]nly subjective delusion could deny that women are capable of practicing vocations other than that of spouse and mother' (*EW*, p. 49). Since the nineteenth-century industrial revolution, the domestic sphere has increasingly become insufficient to engage all the potentialities of women, and employment outside the home is both understandable and, in many instances, desirable. (It is certainly not, however, necessary. Individual circumstances will dictate which choices are better for each woman.).

Stein claims that a woman's professional life outside of the home violates neither the order of nature nor that of grace (*EW*, p. 79). While it is possible both that one's work will detract from family life and that family life may distract from her profession (just as this may occur for any father); nonetheless, one cannot generalize that this always happens. Further, it is Stein's conviction that a professional (for example, a teacher) who is also a mother can bring much to her work. She will have likely developed her motherly instincts, her warmth, and emotional understanding in ways that an unmarried woman may not have. Nonetheless, Stein's suggestions for balancing biological motherhood and professional calling put woman's primary vocation as the maternal one and her secondary role as a ruler, whereas the 'man's primary vocation appears to be that of ruler and the paternal vocation secondary' (however, 'not subordinate to his vocation as ruler but an integral part of it') (*EW*, p. 74).[9]

Characteristic of Stein's life and spirituality is her love of Scripture, and she is clearly at home employing biblical images and archetypes. In at least one essay, she addresses the difficult question of how to interpret many Old and New Testament passages about the relations between men and women (especially, the focus on the headship of the husband [I Corinthians 11 and Ephesians 5:22f.] and Paul's insistence that he will not allow women to speak in church [I Timothy 2]). In several places in 'The Separate Vocations of Man and Woman According to Nature and Grace,' Stein claims that cultural considerations need to play a part in our interpretation of certain passages, and she understands some passages as reflecting the fallen order, not the original or redeemed order. For example, she says:

> [w]hat is said here and what may have been feasible concerning certain improprieties in the Greek community is not to be considered as binding for the principal teaching on the relationship of the sexes. It contradicts too strongly the words and the whole custom of the Lord who had women among his closest companions, and who showed at every turn in His redemptive work that He was as concerned about the soul of woman as the soul of man. [*EW*, p. 69]

Furthermore, some interpretations are in conflict with Paul's own claim that in Christ there is neither male nor female (Galatians 3:28). Thus, Stein insists that great care is necessary in interpreting the passages and we should be attentive to the distinction between the fallen and redeemed orders.

But she also takes seriously the claim that, as Christ is head of the Church, so a husband is head of his wife. As a helpmate and companion, one is subordinate to the tasks of the other, and Stein says that women have a 'natural tendency towards obedience and service'; 'Obedient I feel my soul, always most beautifully free' (*EW*, p. 46). (Stein repeats this sentiment in 'The Marriage of the Lamb,' quoting Goethe's phrase, 'Obedient, my soul felt free indeed,' calling for such obedience in all Christians.) Stein argues, however, that such feminine obedience does not imply any lesser worth or any kind of value judgment. Although Eve was designed as a helpmate, she was as one equal and like Adam.

Thus, Stein does use the language of subordination, but by this she does not mean that women should be subjugated to men, nor does she think that men are superior to women. After quoting the passages of Genesis recording the creation of Eve out of the rib of Adam, Stein says: 'just as the Son issues from the Father, and the Holy Spirit from the Father and the Son, so, too, the woman emanated from man and posterity from them both' (*EW*, p. 62). While there is a kind of preeminence of the man insofar as woman was created out of man, there is no inequality, as there is no inequality among the persons of the Trinity. Inappropriate subjugation of women to men came with the Fall and reflects the fallen order, and our history is certainly filled with examples of fallen versions of male–female relations. Nonetheless, Stein holds out an ideal of redeemed human nature and authentic male–female relations, which are in accord with biblical language and truly fulfill both the feminine and masculine natures.

In addition to struggling with a number of difficult biblical passages, Stein very briefly addresses a further controversial issue: women in the priesthood (see *EW*, pp. 83–5 and pp. 123–4). She says that while it cannot be forbidden by dogma, tradition and the example of Christ both speak against it. Women were deeply and intimately involved in Jesus's ministry; nonetheless, He did not make any women priests. Stein also sees significance in the fact that Christ came to earth as a man, and that significance is reflected in the limitation of the priestly task to men. Whereas women are symbolic of the Church (they are 'called to increase the number of God's children by imparting natural life and the life of grace' [*EW*, pp. 121–2]), men are symbolic of Christ. Stein was clearly, however, in favor of greater involvement of women in the liturgical service. She notes in 1932 that the position of women in the Church had clearly deteriorated. In the early years of the Church, women had positions and official duties as deaconesses, and '[t]he fact that a gradual change took place indicates the possibility of development in an opposite direction' (*EW*, p. 160). Thus, while Stein denies any dogmatic objections to a female priesthood, she does not endorse it. Instead, she sees the call for increased involvement of women as pointing to other tasks.

Stein's general tack for dealing with challenges to the Church is to be open and to consider the objections, but not uncritically. She is in favor of constant reform and improvement, but not of an overthrow of the Church.[10] On the critical and foundational points, the Church is, Stein claims, reliable and offers the standard by which to judge all other things. We can see an example of this approach in her openness to many aspects of the liberal feminist movement and in her insistence that modern research methods proffer much that is useful. She does not endorse uncritical acceptance of new ideas, but she does endorse an impartial consideration of new claims and positions and cites, for example, the way in which the Catholic Women's Movement arose through a careful consideration and selection from the liberal feminist movement. (Stein speaks consistently of the moderate feminist movement with approval. She is, however, wary of some of the philosophical and political foundations of the movement, for example, the influence of German Idealism and political Liberalism. She advocates instead a Catholic feminism building from faith and a Catholic worldview, which nonetheless draws inspiration and insight from the secular movements.)

One challenge to the Church about which she was unambiguously critical, however, was that of National Socialism. Most of Stein's lectures retain a rather objective style, stating her position – not without emotion – but in a quiet, straightforward way that suggests careful consideration of all sides, yet firm conviction. But in her 1932 lectures, one can hear a much more passionate tone. In her Münster lectures from that year, Stein criticizes National Socialism and that 'multitude of thoughtless people satisfied with hackneyed expressions concerning the *weaker sex* or even the *fair sex*' (*EW*, p. 157). She is clearly worried about the rising political party that claimed that women's purpose was merely the bearing of Aryan babies. Such a view, in both its Romantic and biological forms, denies the many and varied achievements and accomplishments of women. It views women, as well as all members of the society, as atoms within a well-ordered mechanistic structure, recognizing neither the organic nature of social patterns nor the unique value of each individual. And it fully lacks an orientation to spirituality and spiritual destiny.

In July of the same year, Stein participated in a meeting of the Association of Catholic Young Women; approximately 7,000 young people gathered, all standing under the banner of the 'White Rose' and publicly protesting against the Third Reich. At the meeting, Stein lectured before a group of a thousand about the task of women as leaders of the youth in the Church – a clear challenge to Hitler's own youth movement. She focused on our understanding of the Body of Christ: we are not primarily members of a family or state, but our first and foremost identity is as members of the Body of Christ. (National Socialism erred on this very point, undermining each person's primary identity as a member of the Body of Christ; furthermore, it also undermined the rights of the family in favor of a stronger state.) Those who belong to Christ also belong to each other; we are one organism, one whole with many diverse members. As such, we must fight against any philosophy that denies the full humanity of women. She concludes that '[y]outh work and particularly work among girls in the name of the Church is perhaps the greatest task to be solved at the present time in Germany' (*EW*, p. 251). Stein's response to National Socialism, as well as the cultural and societal chaos of her era, is to call for full human beings, who resist all that will denigrate, deny, and repress each individual's value and potentialities. And Stein understands the singularity of the feminine to emphasize just such an orientation.[11]

The education of women

Stein's philosophy of women is directly related to her understanding of education. If sexual difference is merely physical, then much of our education need not be affected by it; the life of the mind would be indifferent to the pupil's gender.[12] But if sexual difference involves the entire structure of each person, then intellectual study cannot be indifferent to questions of feminine and masculine natures. Stein takes the latter view, arguing that sexual difference affects the whole structure of the person and, thus, education cannot be neutral regarding the sex of the child. Education, for both men

83

and women, should aim to develop not only their humanity but also their specific masculine or feminine distinctiveness.

When she was younger, Stein would often tutor others in her classes, and she spent at least a decade in full-time teaching. Most of her pedagogical writings focus on the education of women, and she became the intellectual leader for an association of female Catholic teachers and an adviser in educational reform (the Catholic Teachers' Association called Stein 'the hope of Catholic Germany').[13] Throughout her writings and lectures we can see at least three concepts that dominate Stein's pedagogical theory: first, a concern for a proper understanding of our human, feminine or masculine, and individual natures; second, the need for a harmonious education which develops our emotional, intellectual, and physical capacities; and finally, the religious foundation of all formation.

In a 1932 lecture prepared for her courses at Münster, Stein briefly traces the history of women's education in Europe, citing first the Reformation's closing of convents and repudiation of the ideal of virginity. In doing so, one clear avenue for what could count as a successful life for a woman outside of the home was closed (see *EW*, p. 164). The Reformation did, however, emphasize the education of women. Martin Luther (1483–1546) wanted the Bible to be available to and read by all people, including women, and, because of this, there was a demand that the civil authorities make provision for the basic education of women. Unfortunately, that education rarely went beyond an elementary level.

Between 1618 and 1648 (the span of the Thirty Years' War) education in general deteriorated. It was revived, however, with the eighteenth-century Enlightenment, and by the nineteenth century there were public high schools for women. These were, however, under the jurisdiction of men and formed on the model of men's education. Stein cites rather eye-catching explanations which were given for why women should be educated; for example, the First General Meeting of the Headmasters and Teachers of High Schools for Girls (1872) argued, '[i]t is necessary to make available to women the same opportunities for intellectual culture as are available to men. This should be done so that the German husband may not suffer boredom at home by the shortsightedness and narrow-mindedness of his wife' (*EW*, p. 165).

There were certainly protest movements, and Stein refers admiringly to Helene Lange's memoirs.[14] Lange (1848–1939) herself was a moderate in the feminist movement. While she insisted on the liberation of women, the preservation of women from exploitation, their development as persons, and the weaknesses of our masculine Western culture, she did not – in contrast to the radical feminists of the day – deny a distinctive feminine nature. The General Society of German Teachers, founded approximately 40 years prior to Stein's lectures, took up Lange's challenge and advocated improved education for girls, insisting that 'authentic women can be formed only by women' and pushing for improved secondary education (*EW*, p. 167). Lange's movement itself did not succeed, but it did inspire further initiatives, and women were finally allowed to take preparatory courses and the university entrance exams. The first group passed in 1892, and admission into the universities was opened to women in 1901. Full matriculation, however, was not allowed until 1908, just a few years before Stein entered. (These successes did not yet guarantee full professional equality for women. There were still barriers preventing them from taking certain professional examinations and practicing in various professions, not the least of which was as university professor. Stein herself was influential in the opening of university professions to women in 1919.)

In 1930, despite the achievements of the women's movements and the new women's schools opened for both vocational and university training, Stein still sees the situation as critical, and she opens her lecture 'Fundamental Principles of Women's Education' with the claim that '[o]ur entire educational system has been in a state of crisis for decades' (*EW*, p. 129). The problem is a fundamental misunderstanding of the whole concept of education. The Enlightenment model – which was then prevalent in the elementary schools, high schools, and teachers' colleges – focused on imprinting as many facts as possible upon the young minds, as if they were blank slates (*tabulae rasae*) to be written upon. There was a focus on memorization and rote exercise; education meant filling empty minds with information. In contrast, Stein insists that '[e]*ducation* is not an external possession of learning but rather the *gestalt which the human personality assumes under the influence of manifold external forces*' (*EW*, p. 130). Education is formation, not the filling of minds with encyclopedic knowledge. It is 'the orientation of the whole person towards the goal for which he or she is destined' (*EW*, p. 208).

Stein develops the image of the educator as a sculptor: the teacher begins with a child of certain predispositions (both physical and psychological) just as a sculptor begins with a certain kind of material. Education cannot assume that children are blank slates to

85

be written upon, but must recognize that each child has a nature and certain potentialities. The task of the educator is to develop and form the child in accordance with her nature, not to fill an empty mind. The child's development depends, therefore, in large part, upon the degree to which the educators furnish the material necessary for the actualization of the potentials already present, and there must be tasks appropriate for the cultivation of the child's faculties (as 'the faculties develop only through application' [*EW*, p. 132]).

Education is formation, and, Stein claims, only what reaches the soul internally can be a part of formation; what touches merely the senses or intellect, in contrast, is a possession. The soul itself is touched by values, to which we have access through our emotions. Thus, it is legitimate, and even necessary, for emotionally formative subjects to play a central role in education, especially in women's education. Stein is critical of one-sided intellectual development that fails to form the students in this way, and she advocates the regular study of literature, art, and history, all of which appeal to and form our emotional lives. While many values can be introduced in the context of family life, students also need '[a]n adequate introduction to the entire cultural life' and thus the fuller range of values (*EW*, p. 217). The primary tasks of the school are to introduce the students to that whole range of values available through culture and to teach the students how to be receptive to and participate in the world of value.

Education cannot, however, consist simply of such emotional formation (which, moreover, can only be done indirectly, as our responses to value are centered in the personal realm).[15] There must also be development of our intellect and rational capacities. The intellect is the eye of the emotions, and each person must learn to compare, discriminate, weigh and measure. Therefore, right formation requires the development of both our emotional and our intellectual life, and if teachers fail in the latter, we will end up with fanaticism and indiscriminate enthusiasm. Nonetheless, 'the development of intellect may not be increased at the expense of the refinement of emotion' (*EW*, p. 137). It would be turning a mere means into an end in itself.

Education is first of all formation, and 'all educational work, even that imparted through objective forms, aims at personality formation' (*EW*, p. 223). Nonetheless, the training of the intellect is critical, and Stein advocates training both the theoretical and practical intelligence. The former is developed through abstract sciences, for example, mathematics, the theoretical sciences, and pure philosophy; the latter, practical intelligence, is formed through concrete tasks.[16] Stein provides at least two reasons for the training of the practical intelligence. First, '[o]nly where conviction and intention are successfully translated into action can it be shown whether an enthusiasm is legitimate, whether higher things are actually preferred over lower things' (*EW*, p. 137). Therefore, Stein argues that all students – regardless of whether they expect to work in the university or a factory – need to develop the intelligence and judgment necessary for action, for action is the test of conviction. Secondly, the talents, predispositions, and interests of many students will be in less academic fields, and the development of practical intelligence can assist in vocational training. Her view seems to be that both purely intellectual study and more practical application are necessary for all students; most students will, however, want to focus on one or the other, and schools should be prepared to offer assessment and career guidance as well as vocational training.

Education should form the whole person, and a right approach requires a clear anthropology: if one does not know how human beings, both men and women, *should* be, one cannot help them to become that. Thus, education should form our physical bodies and our intellectual capacities (including both the practical and theoretical). The primary aim, however, of all education is the formation of the person and her emotional responsiveness to the world of value. Stein's educational theory, however, like her anthropology, is radically oriented toward the divine, and therefore foremost among the values to which the individual should be responsive are religious ones.

Stein was repeatedly criticized for her inclusion of the spiritual dimension in so many of her lectures. In a letter to a friend, she writes:

I was prepared for resistance in Bendorf [where she gave the lecture 'Fundamental Principles of Women's Education']. I only wish it had been expressed more clearly and less convolutedly. For no one said a word about its being 'too pious,' that is, that they took exception to the radical orientation to the supernatural. But, probably, that was in the background for several, although the discussion was directed to completely different matters. Don't you agree? ... Because of the weeks of total silence since then, I perceived that the rejection was probably stronger [than I had thought], and your kind words confirm it for me. (*Letters*, no.73)

87

Although disappointed by the reception of her claims, she was 'unrepentant' and never ceased arguing that divine grace is the only thing that will heal our wounds at the deepest level. Like St Augustine (354–430), Stein claims that all human beings are fundamentally restless; our hearts are formed to desire God and will be satisfied only in union with the divine.[17] Thus, education, in its task of forming the whole person, should be concerned with our religious lives and spiritual development as well as our intellectual and emotional lives. Stein concludes, however, that a teacher's 'most urgent duty is to open the child's path to God' (*EW*, p. 138). While Stein emphatically states that '*no achievement of the human mind can be dispensed with in the system of girls' education,*' it is the transformations of the human heart, and especially the turn to its Creator, that concern her most deeply (*EW*, p. 220).

Notes

1 Many of these are collected in *EW*. (The first 1987 edition of *EW* includes an essay that is not by Stein; this problem was corrected in the 1996 edition.)

2 At a couple of points Stein criticizes German studies that tried to establish the differences between the sexes through quantitative studies, looking at what occurred on average and calculating the frequency with which various traits appeared in men versus women. Such an approach does little to show whether these differences simply reveal *types*, which are subject to change, or *species*, which are not. In her investigations, Stein is interested in showing that the differences are ones of species, not merely of types.

3 'Edith Stein's Philosophy of Woman and Women's Education' in *Hypatia. A Journal of Feminist Philosophy*, 4.1 (1989): 273.

4 See the 'Diskussion zum Vortrag, Grundlagen der Frauenbildung' in the appendix to *ESGA* 13, p. 246.

5 Stein generally understands the masculine and feminine singularities as complementary. She does argue, however, that – in certain ways – the feminine orientation is more accurate. Human persons are more valuable than objective values, and as Stein points out, '[a]ll truth is discerned by persons; all beauty is beheld and measured by persons. All objective values exist in this sense for persons. And behind all things of value to be found in the world stands the *person of the Creator*' (EW, p. 256). Thus, the personal outlook is actually the most objective, for there is no objective viewpoint other than a personal one.

6 See, for example, Laura Garcia's 'Edith Stein – Convert, Nun, Martyr' in *Crisis* (June 1997): 18–23 and María Ruiz Scaperlanda's *Edith Stein: St Teresa Benedicta of the Cross* (Huntington, IN: Our Sunday Visitor Publishing, 2001, 88–9).

7 'Die Bestimmung der Frau' in *ESGA* 13, p. 50.

8 Following Paul and much of the Catholic tradition, Stein claims that in fact the single life consecrated to God is a higher calling than the married life.

9 Stein again insists that not all women are called to be biological mothers. While, on the whole, marriage and motherhood are primary vocations of most women, this is not true for every individual. Some women may also be called to 'singular cultural achievements, and their talents may be adapted to these achievements' (*EW*, p. 189).

10 This balancing act is necessary for the Church, as Stein argues: '[t]he imperturbability of the Church resides in her ability to harmonize the unconditional preservation of eternal truths with an unmatchable elasticity of adjustment to the circumstances and challenges of changing times' (*EW*, p. 161).

11 Rachel Feldhay Brenner makes this a theme of her text on forms of resistance to the Holocaust. See *Writing as Resistance: Four Women Confronting the Holocaust: Edith Stein, Simone Weil, Anne Frank, Etty Hillesum* (Philadelphia, PA: Pennsylvania State University Press, 1997).

12 A number of thinkers distinguish sex and gender, understanding sex as biological and gender as socially constructed. Stein does not make so sharp a distinction.

13 See Oben's 'An Annotated Edition of Edith Stein's Papers on Woman' (PhD dissertation, Catholic University of America, Washington, DC, 1979), pp. 12ff.

14 *Lebenserinnerungen* (Berlin: F.A. Herbig, 1927).

15 See Chapter 2 above.

16 In a number of places, Stein recommends the Montessori system for such training.

17 In her dissertation, Sr Anselm Mary Madden develops the Augustinian themes in Stein's educational theory. See 'Edith Stein and the Education of Women: Augustinian Themes' (PhD dissertation, St Louis University, St Louis, MO, 1962).

5

Christian Philosophy

During the 1920s and early 1930s, Stein gave lectures for the Catholic circuit and translated Christian texts, and her philosophical writings of the following years reflect these activities, revealing her interest in articulating theoretical positions compatible with traditional Christian dogma and sympathetic to the medieval scholastic tradition.[1] Her primary intellectual formation, however, was as a phenomenologist. One can see throughout her work of this period a clear project of creating a dialogue between more contemporary philosophy and the great medieval Christian tradition.

In the Preface to *Finite and Eternal Being*, Stein acknowledges the influence of Fr Erich Przywara, especially his formidable text *Analogia entis*, and Stein was deeply involved in a number of intellectual projects inspired by Przywara. (Fr Przywara is now little known, but in European Catholic circles of the day, he was a powerful force, editing the journal *Stimmen der Zeit* [Voices of the Time] and in regular exchange with the major theologians, including Karl Barth [1886–1968], Paul Tillich [1886–1965], Hans Urs von Balthasar [1905–88], and Karl Rahner [1904–84].) Although not agreeing on all details, Przywara and Stein shared a vision of integrating phenomenology and scholastic philosophy, and both were concerned about the Church's response to the 'Modernist Crisis.'

Among Catholics in Germany at the turn of the century, there was something of a ghetto mentality: during the late nineteenth century, with Bismarck's (ultimately unsuccessful, although powerful) *Kulturkampf* (culture wars), Catholics were ostracized and, understandably, came to see much of mainstream culture as hostile. Further, between the years 1890 and 1914, the Catholic Church in Europe was embroiled in the Modernist Crisis, battling theologians and intellectuals who embraced (and those who appeared to embrace) German Idealism with its historicist understanding of religion and religious belief. There were certainly dangerous intellectual waters to be negotiated, but – at least in certain quarters – the response to the philosophical challenges was reactionary at best. Both Stein and Przywara, however, saw in the contemporary phenomenological movement resources for responding to German Idealism and an opportunity for Catholic thought to converse with contemporary thought and culture.

All of Stein's works between 1929 and 1936 present such a dialogue. The year 1929 marks the publication of Stein's contribution to the *Festschrift* volume in honor of Husserl's seventieth birthday ('Husserl's Phenomenology and the Philosophy of St Thomas Aquinas' [HT]) and 1936, the completion of *Finite and Eternal Being*. The *Festschrift* article compares Husserl and Aquinas on several philosophical points (including the nature of the philosophical project and a discussion of what can be known and how it is known), pointing out their philosophical compatibilities, although favoring Aquinas where their paths diverge. The article was intended as a first, brief comparison of the two thinkers. Six years later, when Stein wrote *Finite and Eternal Being*, she was no longer interested in a strict comparison. Rather, she presents her own metaphysical positions, which reveal the influence of both phenomenology and medieval scholasticism but are reducible to neither. During the time between the two pieces, Stein attempted once again to obtain a university position and wrote a *Habilitationsschrift*, *Potency and Act*, working through many of the questions which would be more fully developed in *Finite and Eternal Being*.

In this work, Stein develops a vision of philosophy as not only foundational to other intellectual disciplines but also as comprehensive, grasping all of being. Increasingly central to her writing is her conception of Christian philosophy. In all of her work following her conversion, Stein is a Christian thinker; in these texts, however, she is not only a Christian thinker, but also an explicitly Christian philosopher. She offers critiques of the more agnostic Husserlian phenomenology that clearly favor the Christian philosophy of St Thomas (while also noting points of real compatibility between the two), and in *Finite and Eternal Being*, she articulates her understanding of Christian philosophy and develops arguments for the existence of God. Prior to turning to her more metaphysical claims regarding being, essence, and personhood, which are central to her mature synthesis of medieval and contemporary thought (these will be themes in the next chapter), Stein's critical examination of Husserl's phenomenology and claims regarding the nature of Christian philosophy, arguments for the existence of God, and the mark of the Trinitarian God on nature should be considered.

Questions regarding phenomenology

The spirit of the Scholastics certainly imprinted phenomenology, and Husserl was reported as saying that phenomenology 'converges towards Thomism and prolongs Thomism.'[2] After the publication of *Logical Investigations*, Husserl's thought was hailed as the 'new scholasticism.' While these were initial receptions of Husserlian phenomenology, the two schools have not, since then, always been thought to be good bed-fellows. Nonetheless, Stein argues that a primary similarity between Thomas Aquinas and Husserl is their general conception of – and optimism regarding – the philosophical task. Both Thomas and Husserl search for the *logos* and intelligible structure of all that is, and there is a prevailing conviction guiding their philosophical work that 'it is possible for our knowledge to uncover, step by step, more and more about this *logos*, if it takes the lead in conformity with the strictest intellectual honesty' (HT, pp. 130–31/9).

Beyond this general conviction, however, the starting points of the two thinkers differ. In her *Festschrift* article, and again in her comments at Juvisy and in *Potency and Act*,[3] Stein questions Husserl's general project. (She usually presents her critiques as *questions* that Husserl needs to answer, not as direct criticisms. It is possible – and perhaps likely – that he could respond to at least some of her critiques.) Husserlian phenomenology is a method that begins with consciousness, analyzing how experience presents itself to us and moving to a greater understanding of essences, that is, the basic ways in which our experiences are structured. Stein suggests, however, that once transcendental phenomenology (of, for example, Husserl's post-*Logical Investigations* variety) makes the subject or consciousness the philosophical starting point, there is little way to move beyond the subject. She says:

> [t]he world which is constructed in the acts of the subject always remains a world for the subject. It could not succeed in this way –

as was objected again and again to the founder of phenomenology by his circle of pupils – in winning back from the sphere of immanence, that objectivity from which he had proceeded and which it was his aim to safeguard: a truth and reality free from all subject-relativity. With the new interpretation, which was the result of the transcendental inquiry, existence, equated with manifesting itself to a consciousness, will never satisfy the truth-seeking intellect. (HT, p. 136/32)

The orientation of phenomenology to consciousness prevents it, Stein suggests, from achieving the objectivity that Husserl claims it is after.[4] Putting the critique perhaps too simply: she fears that, using the phenomenological method, I will not get the real world but merely the world as it appears to me. While Husserl was clearly not a relativist, Stein worried that his method may end up in the very idealism that Husserl set out to fight.

In Thomas's writings, in contrast, the realist thesis is never suspended; St Thomas never advocates bracketing the existence of the world. He is not interested in analyzing possible worlds; rather, his philosophy searches for 'the most complete image of *this* world' (HT, p. 144/62). Thus, while both Thomas and Husserl search for essences and essential structures, Thomas does not look for them as the condition for possible worlds but rather as a way to investigate this world.

In a similar way, phenomenology can only be oriented toward objective truth as a regulative ideal. Husserl cannot posit the existence of objective truth, or the whole truth, without compromising the transcendental method. In contrast, for Thomas, the whole truth exists and is not merely an ideal regulating his search. The whole truth is the world as divinely known. (Furthermore, because there is a divine knower, revelation is possible. Therefore, Thomas argues that while natural reason can get us to truth, it is not the only path. Both Thomas and Husserl agree that the whole truth is that toward which natural reason leads, but Thomas's claim that the whole truth is a real rather than a regulative ideal broadens the possible sources by which we acquire truth.)

For Husserl, objective truth functions as the goal toward which reason leads. Thomas agrees that *ratio* or reason aims at truth; however, he separates *ratio* into natural and supernatural reason, a distinction Husserl does not make.[5] In making this distinction, Thomas insists that there is a limit to our natural reason. We can and must use our faculties, and we can no more free ourselves from our intellectual faculties than we can escape our shadows. But our reason is not supernatural reason, and any attempt (such as Kant's, for example) to find the limits of reasons from within and by means of human reason itself are problematic. They lack, so it appears, an Archimedean point outside ourselves from which to ask the question about our own limits. Because he begins in consciousness and limits himself to that one field, Husserl cannot provide a critique of the limits of reason. There is no point from which to conduct such a critique, whereas for Aquinas, such a principle exists in the thesis of God. (Aquinas does not place God first in the 'order of knowing'; however, God is first in the 'order of being.' Stein implies that this might offer a point from which to critique human reason, understanding the limits of reason through study of revelation.)

The bulk of Stein's critique was written for the 1929 *Festschrift*, and it does not appear again in *Finite and Eternal Being*. In the latter work, her concerns turn away from the evaluation of these two thinkers to the positive task of articulating her own metaphysical claims. Some scholars have suggested that in presenting her own views, Stein abandoned phenomenology and turned instead to Thomism, motivated perhaps by 'docility to the magisterium.'[6] But her study of scholastic thought and adoption of Thomistic categories cannot be read as a simple replacement of phenomenology with the more explicitly Christian philosophy of St Thomas. While Stein found phenomenology lacking as she attempted to articulate the theoretical bases for Christian doctrine, she also frequently chose phenomenological approaches over scholastic ones. Thus, rather than reading her as a phenomenologist turned Thomist, it is more accurate to see her as a thinker trained in the phenomenological method who began seriously studying and integrating scholastic thought into her work, using it to supplement the shortcomings she found in phenomenology. Nonetheless, her vision of the philosophical project differs significantly from her earlier view, and she argues in her later writings for a distinctively Christian philosophy.

The nature of Christian philosophy

Stein dedicates the final section of the opening chapter of her opus *Finite and Eternal Being* to a discussion of the nature of Christian philosophy. For many, the idea of 'Christian philosophy' is contradictory. If it is Christian, it depends upon revealed truths; if it is philosophy, it cannot appeal to any special revelation but only to what is accessible through natural experience and reason. Even

Thomas Aquinas argues that when one moves from natural reason to belief, one also moves from philosophy to theology. Stein, however, insists that there is a way to understand 'Christian philosophy' that is both Christian and philosophical.

Stein begins by employing Jacques Maritain's distinction between the nature and condition of philosophy.[7] The first, the nature, refers to the nature of philosophy *per se*, that is, as a discipline using only natural reason and experience. According to their natures, philosophy and theology differ. But philosophy is also a historical science, developing within time and under various historical conditions. Given a Christian context of development, one may have a Christian *condition* of philosophy. Christianity would then offer categories and concepts which may be scrutinized philosophically.

One example of such a Christian condition for philosophy would be medieval Europe, which developed under the undeniable influence of Christianity. Many of the philosophical tasks and questions arose in relation to and conjunction with theological concerns, and terms arising originally from revelation came to have philosophical significance. Stein's favorite examples of this are the notions of *creature* and *Creator*. Compare, for example, an understanding of this world as created with an interpretation that sees this world as simply here or, as Aristotle did, as eternal. The doctrine of creation, coming from faith, may have been the occasion for looking at our experience anew; one can, however, look away from revelation as such and analyze the claims purely philosophically.

Likewise, theological claims put before philosophy questions it otherwise may have been unlikely to consider, including the problem of two natures in one person and one nature and three persons. From these questions, philosophical concepts such as *person* versus *nature* were developed. Thus, revealed truths such as God's creation *ex nihilo*, the Incarnation, and the Trinity provide ways to understand natural experience and can be a motive for making distinctions that might not otherwise have been made. In this, however, the philosopher must articulate and defend these concepts not only as a believer but also as a philosopher, and the conclusions of these analyses then become the philosophical 'goods' of all later philosophy.

Philosophy has, however, changed significantly since the Middle Ages. For Thomas, philosophy was a discipline covering much that a twentieth- or twenty-first-century person would consider part of another field. We now make more divisions among the tasks allotted to natural reason, distinguishing biology, physics, political science, psychology, and sociology. The task now allotted to philosophy, as Stein understands it, is not the performance of any one of these sciences but, rather '[t]he clarification of the foundations of all the sciences' (*EeS*, pp. 19–20). As such, it aims to articulate the nature of *being* itself (regardless of whether it is the being of an ant or a cantaloupe), the construction of beings as such, and the essential division of the beings according to species and genera.[8]

In light of this goal of clarifying the foundations of all the sciences and articulating the nature of being itself, Stein sees a further way to understand the relationship of philosophy and revealed truths. If, she argues, the philosopher wishes to remain faithful to his or her goal of understanding being itself and the fundamental structure of all being *and* the philosopher is convinced of the truths of faith, believing that there are certain truths accessible only through revelation, then such a thinker cannot limit his or her work simply to what is accessible through natural means (*EeS*, p. 23). If something is made visible to the thinker through a higher Light, then it is unreasonable to attempt to understand the ultimate structure of reality depending only on what is known through one's own light, especially when convinced that it is indeed a meager light. What has been revealed is not simply incomprehensible. It is intelligible in itself and intelligible to us in the measure to which we have been given light to see.

Thus, Stein argues, if a philosopher wishes to understand being in all its fullness and depth, then he or she cannot remain simply within mere natural reason but, rather, must enrich her philosophy with theology, without it, however, becoming theology. She distinguishes the two tasks, claiming that

> [i]f it is the task of theology to establish the facts of revelation as such and to work out their proper meaning and connection, then it is the task of philosophy to bring into harmony what it has worked out by its own means with that which it has borrowed from belief and theology. (*EeS*, p. 24)

If philosophy stops before a question that it cannot answer with its own resources (for example, the origin of the human soul) and uses belief as a source of knowledge, then it is no longer a pure and autonomous philosophy. Stein does not think, however, that it is then right to call it *theology*. She suggests an analogy: one can write a historical work about physics without writing a book that would be classified as 'natural science'; likewise, one can write a philosophical book including theology without thereby doing theology. She adds, however, one qualification: there is clearly a disanalogy here insofar as the historian does not ask about the veracity of the physicists' claims, whereas the philosopher takes the claims of faith *as true*. Nonetheless, in both cases the researcher in the one field expands his work by including the claims from another field and may only proceed in his own work with those claims. Stein warns that the philosopher must acknowledge the loan from faith and cannot claim that they are her own, independent conclusions, but one may, nonetheless, think philosophically with claims from faith. Quoting Przywara, she says, 'philosophy is completed "*through* theology, not *as* theology" ' (*EeS*, p. 26).

Christian philosophy, thus understood, aims at a comprehensive understanding of being as a unity 'which natural reason *and* revelation make accessible to us' (*EeS*, p. 27). The *summae* of the medieval thinkers have such a goal, and, she argues, all human knowing by nature aims at such completion, to know all that can be known. An unbeliever will take the truths of faith included in philosophy as 'hypotheses' rather than 'theses,' as the believer will understand them. Nonetheless, if one proceeds honestly, acknowledging what is borrowed from faith, one may continue to do philosophy while also incorporating truths of faith. And if both the author and the reader are as free of prejudices as, in their philosophical conviction they should be, then neither will shrink from such an attempt.

Defending the existence of God

We can see an example of such philosophical honesty in Stein's argument for the existence of God. It is not a *proof per se* for God's existence, but an argument pointing to one place where we gain the concept of God and then arguing that it is reasonable to believe in God. But she also acknowledges quite openly that her 'argument' requires a leap of faith; a believer will easily jump the chasm, whereas the unbeliever will stop before it (*EeS*, p. 107).

In the final section of Chapter 2 of *Finite and Eternal Being*, Stein begins by limiting herself to the phenomenological sphere, the realm of consciousness. She says that the fact of our own being is undeniable and that we have an unreflexive self-awareness. Even if we are deceived about all else, we cannot be deceived about our own being. Our being, however, is temporal and always in the tension between being and non-being. The ego has a longing, however, 'not only for the endless continuation of its being, but also for the full possession of being' (*EeS*, p. 54). Thus, we come to the idea of the fullness of being. We ourselves do not have that being, but we taste it in our temporal existence and long for the full possession of being. In this idea of a *pure being*, that is, one that neither gains nor loses its being but always has the fullness of being, we have the idea of God. Thus, we can get the idea of an eternal being from the temporal passage of experiences, leading us to the idea of something without such becoming and passing away, but which *is* fully.

Similarly, Stein approaches the same argument from a slightly different angle. She says that we live in a 'now' suspended between what is already and what is not-yet, yet we *are* in each moment. In any moment, we have something of the fullness of being, albeit only momentarily. In this momentary fullness, we find an image of the eternal, albeit a very weak and distant image, and the conscious I is, therefore, (very distantly) analogous to the Eternal.

It has frequently been argued by various contemporary philosophers that belief in God is not only incapable of proof but also unreasonable.[9] Stein challenges this claim by drawing an analogy between our trust in a support for our being and a child's trust in her mother. In *Being and Time*, Martin Heidegger describes *angst* as the basic human emotion; we have, he says, a fear of nothingness, of death, of ceasing to be. The avoidance of angst is an avoidance of an authentic attitude toward life; it is a kind of self-deception and inauthentic mode of being. In contrast, Stein writes quite adamantly, '[a]ngst is certainly not ordinarily the ruling life feeling' (*EeS*, p. 56). Only in cases of illness is angst such a foundational feeling. Our ordinary experience is one of confidence and a great security about our own being. While it is true that we can and do hide our own finitude from ourselves, our security in being is not merely the result of self-deception. Just as a child is not *unreasonable* in trusting that her mother will not drop her, so too our confidence in our own being is not an unreasonable assumption. Death will come, but our lives, in order to be authentic, need not be ordered by an angst in the face of our own inability to maintain ourselves in being.

Stein continues, however, that this appropriate confidence is analogous to the child's confidence in a further respect: the reason the child is secure is that she has a strong arm upholding her; so too do we have a support and ground for our being. We are not the source of our own being, but the overwhelming fact of our confidence suggests that there is such a support. Stein puts forward two paths by which people understand that support and ground to be the

Eternal Being: (1) the way of faith and (2) the way of reason, using proofs for God's existence.

In the previous arguments, Stein simply argued that there are sources within consciousness and our immediate experience from which to gain the *idea* of God. In the final section of Chapter 2, she develops a slightly stronger argument for God's existence, adapting Aquinas's 'third way.'[10] She argues that we – and all finite things – are contingent and therefore must receive our being and existence from somewhere else, and in making this argument she points both to our need to be placed in existence and to be maintained in existence. Clearly, the I is not identical with the Eternal Being because there are holes in our knowledge, mysteries regarding where we come from and where we are going (she quotes Heidegger, claiming that we find ourselves thrown into being). We are not the origin of our own being and thus must receive it. But such a 'reception of being independent of an eternal being is unthinkable' because there is nothing outside of an eternal being that possesses its own being (*EeS*, p. 53). It could be that my flowing being has a ground in something finite. The finite, however, cannot be the final support and ground. We are more confident about our continuance in being than such a limited support suggests; '[t]he security of being that is felt in my flowing being points to an *immediate* anchoring in the final support and ground of my being (notwith-standing the possible mediating supports)' (*EeS*, p. 58). This feeling is a dark feeling and hardly counts as *knowledge*, but it nonetheless does suggest strongly that there is something more than finite supports.

While Stein's argument for the existence of God is given with a much more tentative note than most traditional arguments, she is nonetheless quite willing to discuss God in her philosophical works. The believing philosopher should use all sources of truth, not simply those accessible to natural reason, in attempting to understand being – given that she makes clear when she is using truths of revelation.

Trinitarian aspects of being

One of the most significant Christian elements that Stein incorpo-rates into *Finite and Eternal Being* is the doctrine of the Trinity. She asks, '[i]f the Creator is the archetype of creation, should we then not find in creation a reflection (even if still a distant one) of the three-in-oneness of Original Being? And should not a deeper understanding of finite being be gained from that?' (*EeS*, p. 328).

Chapter 7 of *Finite and Eternal Being* is dedicated to the image of the Trinity in creation, and she claims that all of creation has the mark of the Trinitarian God. For example, she sees human beings as unities of body, soul, and spirit; angels as unities of spiritual matter,[11] essence, and carrier; and being itself as divided into three types (these will be discussed in the next chapter). Likewise, in her description of spirit as a going-out-of-itself, we see a reflection of the Trinity. She says that God as the 'I am' is also an 'I give myself wholly to a You,' 'am one with a You,' and therefore a 'We are' (*EeS*, p. 324). The interior life of the Trinity is love and self-surrender, and Stein similarly claims that at the root of all creation is communion and community.

Stein's vision of being is thus deeply Trinitarian and deeply communal, and the final chapter of *Finite and Eternal Being* culminates with a discussion of our unity in the Body of Christ. (The chapter is titled 'The Meaning and Foundation of Being Individual,' yet her discussion of being individual ends in a description of the ways in which we are fundamentally communal.) Being a member of the human race is the foundation for being a member of the Mystical Body of Christ, although recognizing that membership requires maturity and growth. We begin by understanding ourselves as members of our families, of small communities, and of a state, seeing other communities as foreign and even dangerous. Only by recognizing our membership in humanity as a whole do we come to see no other person as foreign; this insight, further, 'binds us to human beings of all times and heavenly realms, despite all differences,' and enriches us through contact with differently formed humanity (*EeS*, p. 466).

This claim regarding our fundamental unity is foundational for making sense of the Christian doctrines of the Fall, the Incarnation, and Grace. Salvation history is the history of humanity, and our participation in humanity is what enables it to become our personal story. In summarizing Stein's position, Regina van den Berg says:

> [w]ere it not for the presupposition that all humanity is one, and that man belongs by nature to the community of humanity, then original sin, whereby in one man, all have sinned, would be entirely unintelligible. Adam acted *as* a member of humanity; therefore, his act affects all the members.[12]

Likewise, if all were not one, it would make no sense for *one* man's act to save humanity. Christ participated in humanity and, only thus, could save humanity. Further, His grace 'radiates out to the members because they are united already *from nature* with the Head and are capable – as spiritual beings and in virtue of their free self-opening – to take within themselves His divine life' (*EeS*, p. 478). All human beings are united from nature, Stein claims, and we may be further united, through grace, in the Mystical Body of Christ. This Body is what makes possible the Christian story as a series of historical events that are relevant for all human beings, regardless of how remote their lives may seem to be from the original parents or the Jewish carpenter.

Stein explicitly defends a notion of Christian philosophy incorporating both natural reason and revelation. And although critical of Husserl's transcendental philosophy, she develops her argument for the existence of God (albeit a non-traditional understanding of such an argument) beginning with the phenomenological starting point, the immediate experience of our own consciousness. Her project is, as she somewhat sheepishly admits in the Foreword to her opus, an unabashedly comprehensive one, attempting to understand all of being with the help of whatever truth is available. Thus, she draws from phenomenology and contemporary philosophy, the medieval tradition, revelation, and, as her discussions of matter in Chapter 4 of *Finite and Eternal Being* reveal, even from the latest science. Stein does not quote Justin Martyr's famous saying, but her work reveals a resounding affirmation that 'all truth is God's truth.'

Notes

1 The medieval scholastic tradition was a dominant school of thought in medieval Europe, contrasted most frequently with the monastic tradition. Prime examples of scholastic thinkers include St Thomas Aquinas and John Duns Scotus.

2 Quoted in, for example, Elisabeth de Miribel's *Edith Stein: 1891–1942* (Paris: Éditions du Seuil, 1954), p. 73.

3 See 'Exkurs über den transzendentalen Idealismus', in *Potenz und Akt: Studien zu einer Philosophie des Seins* (Freiburg: Herder, 1998), pp. 246–58.

4 In a review of Husserl's transcendental phenomenology, Stein states the question slightly differently. Husserl distinguishes the cogito or constituting I from the constituted objects. Can, however, the I which constitutes be named a *being* [*Seiendes*] in any way analogous to the beings constituted?

5 In describing this difference, Stein qualifies the contrast, saying, 'Husserl would certainly object that what he understands under reason

lies beyond the opposition of "natural" and "supernatural"; that these are empirical distinctions' (HT, p. 131/10). Husserl speaks of reason as such, 'that which – without prejudice to all empirical distinctions – must be realized everywhere that the discourse by reason is to be meaningful' (HT, p. 131/10).

6 See, for example, Reuben Guilead's *De la Phénoménologie à la Science de la Croix: l'itineraire d'Edith Stein* (Louvain: Nauwelaerts, 1974). The phrase 'docility to the magisterium' is from Ralph McInerny's article 'Edith Stein and Thomism' in John Sullivan (ed.), *Edith Stein Teresian Culture* (Washington, DC: ICS Publications, 1987), p. 81. The Catholic Church has often enjoined study of the writings of St Thomas Aquinas (see, for example, Pope Leo XIII's *Aeterni Patris*).

7 The French philosopher Jacques Maritain (1882–1973) is best known for his work on Thomas Aquinas and is considered a leader in the Thomistic revival. When Stein was in Juvisy, near Paris, for a conference in 1931, she met Maritain and his wife. The three of them became friends, and a number of letters between them have been published. See *Lettres d'Edith Stein. Textes de Raïssa Maritain* (Papers of Jacques Maritain, 25, December 1992) and 'Vier Briefe Edith Steins an Jacques Maritain' in *Katholische Bildung*, 94 (1993): 581–4.

8 For many contemporary thinkers, and certainly for the early phenomenologists, the question regarding *being* was first and foremost about the *intelligibility* of beings. Their question was epistemological, about our knowledge, rather than metaphysical, about existence. In *EeS*, Stein wants to move through the epistemological question to the metaphysical one.

9 Stein addresses this point in a number of places, clearly concerned about this criticism of faith. More recently, in the later part of the twentieth century, defences of the rationality of religious belief have blossomed in the philosophy of religion. See, for example, the work of Alvin Plantinga.

10 See *Summa theologica* I, q. 2, art. 3.

11 Thomas argued that angels do not have matter; they are pure spirits. In contrast, Stein posits a spiritual matter for angels – not a space-filling matter, but a determinable indeterminacy. See *EeS* VII, §5, 6 and VII, §6.

12 'Community in the Thought of Edith Stein', p. 272.

6

Metaphysics and Epistemology of the Later Work

Stein's final major philosophical piece, *Finite and Eternal Being* (*Endliches und ewiges Sein* [*EeS*]), is nearly 500 pages, plus two substantial appendices which were published separately. The work brings together the medieval metaphysical tradition (relying heavily on Thomas Aquinas and John Duns Scotus), Carmelite spirituality, the phenomenological tradition (especially the works of Husserl's students, Hedwig Conrad-Martius, Jean Héring, and Martin Heidegger), and the surprising and rarely acknowledged influence of G.W.F. Hegel. Stein's project in *Finite and Eternal Being* is both extremely ambitious and quite humble. She opens with the words: '[t]his book was written by a student for fellow students' (*EeS*, p. viii). Yet her goal is to gain a comprehensive vision of being, incorporating both philosophical and theological concerns and insights, and central to her vision is the synthesis of contemporary philosophy and medieval thought.

Contemporary philosophy, however, is conducted under very different conditions than those operative for the Christian writers in the Middle Ages. Although philosophy was for many of the medieval thinkers strictly distinguished from theology, revelation was, nonetheless, a measuring-stick used to test the thinkers' conclusions and Christian concerns regularly shaped the philosophers' projects. Philosophy was the 'handmaiden of theology.' In contrast, most nineteenth- and twentieth-century thinkers saw philosophy as an autonomous science that is neither subject to, nor a servant for, theology. This change in approach led to two camps that, especially in the prewar German academy, had nothing to do with one another:

modern philosophy and Catholic philosophy, the heir of the medieval project. The latter came to be seen as a stiff system of concepts, lacking the stream of life and out of touch with the movement of contemporary thought. (Not only did modern and Catholic philosophy have little to do with each other intellectually, they also, quite literally, did not speak the same languages. Prior to Stein's translation of *De veritate* [On Truth], Thomas Aquinas's text had not been available in German. If one were a Thomist, one read Latin; if one were not, she did not read Thomas. With her translation of *De veritate*, Stein made Thomas's thought available to modern philosophers, and she further facilitated this reconciliation by including brief commentary throughout in the translation.)

Although still distinct camps, Stein saw hope in the 1930s for greater communication between the Catholic and the more contemporary schools of philosophy. Modern philosophy was moving away from materialism (Stein cites the works of Edmund Husserl, Max Scheler, Hedwig Conrad-Martius, and Martin Heidegger as examples of this) and thereby away from a position antithetical to Catholic thought, and there was a rebirth and revitalization of medieval philosophy among a group that came to be known as the existential and transcendental Thomists (including Jacques Maritain [1882–1973], Etienne Gilson [1884–1978], and Joseph Maréchal [1878–1944]). Stein was convinced that together, if the contemporary and the traditional schools of philosophy could learn to speak similar philosophical (and literal!) languages, they could find paths to greater truth.

In attempting this synthesis Stein begins with a modern project, the analysis of consciousness, and moves gradually to the more medieval concerns of being and the transcendentals (that is, attributes or properties coextensive with being), trying to show throughout how one can reach more classically Christian positions regarding act and potency, matter and form, and the nature of persons from a contemporary philosophical starting point. It is not possible to look at all of Stein's arguments in *Finite and Eternal Being*, but the key claims include her view of the person, which leads her to adapt the traditional Thomistic and Aristotelian understanding of matter and form, her understanding of being as tripartite, her theory of individuality, and her epistemology, which draws heavily from the contemporary phenomenological tradition. Throughout *Finite and Eternal Being*, Stein appropriates many Thomistic concepts, yet also departs from Thomas, developing a more Scotist model of persons and being.

Matter and form

In both *Potency and Act* and *Finite and Eternal Being*, Stein follows the Aristotelian–Thomist tradition in claiming that the soul is the form of the body, and describing corporeal, animate things (for example, oak trees, armadillos, and anteaters) as unities of matter and form. In this tradition, form is understood as the structure of the thing and the principle of its being and growth.[1] Matter is that which is formed.[2] Consider, for example, a statue of Socrates. The form would be the structure or shape of Socrates; this could be contrasted with the matter – plastic, marble, or bronze. The same form could be in different matter, and one might have plastic, marble, and bronze statues of Socrates, all of which would be recognizable as Socrates. The form of Socrates could not exist without some matter in which it is formed, but one can nonetheless distinguish the form from the matter which is formed.

While this illustration makes the point, it is also slightly misleading. Thomas's primary models for form are not artificial structures, such as a statue of Socrates, but living things, such as trees and squirrels. One distinguishes matter and form in living things by looking at their development over time. Take, for example, a dog. It starts out small as a puppy, consumes its mother's milk and eventually solid food, transforming the food into itself. The matter or body is constantly changing as it sheds fur, loses cells, and absorbs nutrients, creating new fur, bones, and blood. The form or soul, however, is constant, continually making this dog a larger version of the same thing. It is that which drives the development and shapes the matter according to its own image. (The Aristotelian–Thomistic tradition with its *hylomorphism* can be contrasted with both *dualism* and *materialism*.[3] Dualists understand matter and form, or body and soul, not as two interrelated principles, but as two distinct and fully separable parts of human beings. In contrast, materialists deny that there is any thing or principle in human beings other than matter.)

The Aristotelian and Thomistic concept of form has played an important role in Western thought. Both Aristotle and Thomas thought that all members of one species (e.g., human beings) have identical fundamental structures or forms, and the differences among human beings arise from our different matter, conditions of development, and experiences. We are, however, at base, identical in structure. Each human being has the human form and is thus like all other human beings, despite cultural, temporal, intellectual, or religious differences. The notion of a species-form is useful for defending certain universal ethical claims, especially in the natural law tradition, has provided a strong basis for a political democracy, and has been employed to articulate Christian doctrine. For example, the notion of form allows one to make ethical judgments about what all human beings should (or should not) do. Certain acts can be seen as right (or as wrong) for each and every person because we all share in a common humanity that determines that some acts are good (or bad) for *all* of us. Likewise, with a strong notion of a common form, we can say that Jesus became human and thus became essentially like each and every person regardless of race, gender, or historical distance.

Stein follows in this tradition; she strongly affirms a common human form and understands the substantial form, or most basic form, as that shaping the matter of each living thing. In the hylomorphic tradition, however, form has played a double role: it both drives the development and contains the goal of that development. While sympathetic to the notion of form, Stein is dissatisfied with the attempts to give this dual role to a single principle. As she argues, living things are always in the process of coming-to-be and passing-away, yet what it means to be a full dog or a full human being does not come into being or pass away. Finite, real beings are, according to Stein, primarily characterized as beings that do not possess their own being but, rather, need time in order to acquire full being (*EeS*, p. 60). But what it means to be a human or a dog, in contrast, is atemporal, needing no time to come into being (although it might require time for us to understand what it means to be a full human being or to become that ourselves).

Rather than giving these two roles to one principle, Stein – in contrast to Thomas and Aristotle – distinguishes the form in its becoming (which she calls the *Wesensform*) from the form as an essential structure (which she often refers to as the *Wesen* or *Was*). (I would translate *Wesensform* as 'substantial form'; *Wesen* as 'essence,' and *Was* as 'what' or quiddity.) Stein argues that this distinction between form as principle of development and form as goal of development is necessary in order to account for the growth of living, organic beings; it is precisely because we carry the goal with us (in our essential structure) that we can realize that goal in time. And only in relation to the goal can we say that something is incomplete or deficient in some way. Such incompleteness or deficiency lies in the gap between the thing as it is and its goal.

Thus, in contrast to Thomas and Aristotle, Stein posits three principles as basic to all finite, living beings: (1) substantial form or the form as it unfolds in time; (2) matter; and (3) the essence or nature (see EeS, pp. 449–50). The substantial form is that which forms us, acting as a principle of growth; the matter is what is formed; and the essence is the goal of the development. (In this division in our structure, we can see again an echo of the Trinitarian God. Christian orthodoxy declares that in God there is one nature and three persons. Stein interprets this as a 'unity of substance' and a 'triad of carriers' [EeS, p. 329].[4] In a distantly analogous way, each human being has both a nature, making us human, and a carrier of that nature, a substantial form, making us persons. She warns, however, that the analogy is only rough and partial – as is appropriate for created beings that only incompletely reflect the Eternal.) Stein argues, however, that not only are human beings tripartite in structure, so too is all of being.

Being as tripartite

One of the most significant twentieth-century philosophical texts is Martin Heidegger's *Being and Time*, published in 1927. Heidegger opens this work with a call to renew the question of the meaning of being. In *Finite and Eternal Being*, Stein takes up this challenge, presenting a tripartite understanding of being, and her claims regarding substantial form and essence can be best clarified by looking at her theory of being.

'Being' is often thought to be quite obvious and easy to understand; things either exist and therefore have being, or fail to exist. Stein, however, argues that it is not nearly so clear what it means to exist; there are many different kinds of being and ways 'to exist.' In *Finite and Eternal Being*, she presents three main categories of being: real being (*wirkliches Sein*), mental being (*gedankliches Sein*), and essential being (*wesenhaftes Sein*) (*EeS*, Chapter 3 III). She says of each: things as they are efficacious in the world have real being; thoughts have mental being; and atemporal essences and the essential structures of entities have essential being. The first would include a cat as it bats its toy mouse; the second would be the cat and its mouse as remembered or imagined; and the third includes cat-ness and toy-mouse-ness: it is that which makes my thought, the thought *of a cat and his toy*.

Of the three, essential being is in need of the most explanation. In positing this category, Stein insists that there are ideal objects that do not operate under space–time conditions but, nonetheless, are not simply invented by human imagination. They have an independent and consistent meaning that is distinct from existing, 'real' things, yet they are not merely mental beings insofar as they are not reducible to our thoughts. We can talk intelligently about triangles or thousand-sided figures even if these geometric shapes never exist in the empirical world, and there is a structure and logic to these figures independent of our thoughts such that someone can be wrong about their properties and attributes. Stein claims that in order for this to be possible, the structures must have some kind of *being*. They do not exist in time and space as cats and bats do, but rather they have a kind of being appropriate to atemporal entities.

These stable, atemporal structures include, however, not only ideal geometrical objects, but also structures experienced in our everyday lives. Consider, for example, joy. One may be joyful about finishing a project or about receiving some good news or about an upcoming wedding. The duration, intensity, and object motivating the joy differ in each case, but all three are experiences of *joy*. Stein argues that the three are experiences of joy because they all share the same essential structure that distinguishes these experiences from experiences of sadness, depression, contentedness, or any other kind of experience. Furthermore, while it is certainly true that any particular experience of joy unfolds in time, the essential structure of joy does not. The essential structure is *that which* unfolds, and in its essential being, joy itself is timeless, although temporally realized in each instance of joy.

Heidegger's answer to the question of the meaning of Being, put simplistically, is that being is revealed in *Da-sein*'s (i.e., a human being's) engagement with the world; being for Heidegger is time and temporality. Stein's response to the same question is: being is revealed through the search for meaning. Heidegger focuses on our thrown-ness into the world and our projection of future possibilities, and we are anxious in the face of the realization that we do not ground our own being and must make our way in this contingent and uncertain world. While not denying either our thrown-ness or our need to project possibilities, Stein has a greater confidence in the ultimate grounding and intelligibility of the world. Human life is best interpreted as *Da-sein* (being-there) in search of intelligibility; this intelligibility is found, according to Stein, in a thing's essential being, in the essential and eternal structures of meaning.

Stein ultimately identifies essences and essential being with the divine ideas. Ideal objects are grounded and have unity and order in the divine intellect (and, since essential being is rooted in God, all search for meaning is implicitly a search for God). The subtitle of *Finite and Eternal Being* can be translated as 'an attempt at an ascent to the meaning of being'; this can be read both as her attempt to grasp the meaning of being and through her claim that meaning offers a way to reach God in the ascent through essential being to its Eternal ground.

Despite Stein's regular compliments of Thomas Aquinas, it is clear that her position regarding essential structures and their atemporal being goes beyond the moderate realism of Thomas. Stein certainly agrees with Thomas in her general position, but in the details they differ, and on the nature of being, Stein comes closer to the position of John Duns Scotus than Thomas Aquinas. Stein's position can be clarified by looking at three general positions regarding essences, or, as they are often called, universals, and then three further positions within one camp, the realists'.

The three major positions regarding essences are: nominalism, conceptualism, and realism. The *nominalists* accept only universal names but no universal (that is, identical in content) concepts or things. Thus, a nominalist would argue that there is no one thing that it means to be a tree or an experience of joy, nor is there a single structure identical in all human beings. We might have a few traits that are more and less similar, but there is no fundamental structure that is identical in every human being. The *conceptualists* recognize a universality of concepts, but – like the nominalists – they claim that there is nothing in reality which corresponds to these universal concepts.[5] (Thus, a conceptualist would argue that we can have the concept of tree or of joy, but there is nothing such as 'tree-ness' or 'joy' identical in all particular leaves or experiences of joy.) Finally, the *realists* believe that there are in reality natures that correspond to the universal names and concepts. Thus, they would argue for both the concept of tree and a structure – tree-ness – that all individual trees possess; it is that which makes all the particulars, examples of a tree.

Both Stein and Thomas are clearly realists. Stein further distinguishes, however, three groups within the realist camp. First, an *exaggerated realism*, which she identifies with the common interpretation of Plato, claims that there are universals existing somewhere outside of minds and the things of our everyday life. (For the Plato of the middle dialogues, this is the World of the Forms, where the original exemplars of things exist.) Secondly, she points to a line of thought identified with John Duns Scotus, who taught 'a being of the universal in things' (*EeS*, p. 94). Finally, there is a *moderate realism* associated with Aristotle, Boethius (480–c. 525), Anselm (1033–1109), and Thomas Aquinas. This group distinguishes the content of the essence or universal from its mode as a universal. The same content may be in an individual thing or in the mind (that is, in a tree or in the thought of a tree), but the mode of universality can only exist in a mind. Thus, 'universal' comes to mean 'predicable of many things,' although as a content (in either things or in an individual thought), the universal is always individual precisely because it is invariably this universal or that one. One does not have a thought of a universal, but the thought of an individual concept (for example, tree-ness) that is applicable to many things in the world.

Stein identifies herself with the second, the Scotist group. While Stein agrees with the distinction the moderate realists make between the content and mode of the universal, she insists that thoughts of universals or essences are in some significant way different from other thoughts. She says, '[j]ust this, which can be in differing ways and which one can grasp when looking away from its differing ways of being, appears to me to be that which we have up to now named the *essential what*' (*EeS*, p. 97). My consideration of joy itself, the structure of joy, is different from my consideration of a particular joyful experience. Likewise, thoughts of particular friends are different from the thought of the human structure. But in order to be so different, these latter thoughts must, Stein argues, have a different kind of being. Thus, she claims that the thought of joy itself or the human essence, while a thought with mental being, also has essential being.

Thus, Stein rejects moderate realism because it does not strongly enough distinguish various *ways* of being in a mind. There is, she insists, a kind of being common to both the cat and my thought of a cat, guaranteeing that my thought is a thought *of a cat*. That kind of being is the essential being that is present in both the real being of the existing cat and the mental being of my thought of the cat.

Individuality

Stein departs from the Aristotelian–Thomistic tradition in strongly separating the essence (which has essential being) from the substantial form (which has real being and is in the process of realizing the essence). She further departs by insisting that the final determination of form (for humans) is not the species-form but an individual form (see, for example, *EeS*, p. 439). In making this claim, Stein does not deny that we all share a common human structure. There is, she strongly insists, a common human form; nonetheless, Stein repeats the claim made in the earlier phenomenological works that, while all our forms are human ones, there are also individual, formal differences.[6] Thus, while many people share the same qualities, each has that quality in an individual way, and 'the friendliness or goodness of Socrates is different from that of another human being' (*EeS*, p. 151). Each of us has an individual stamp, lying within our soul and imprinting all that we do.[7]

This theme appears in nearly all of her works, from her earliest phenomenological texts, her political works and writings on women, into her Thomistic texts, and the final works on spirituality. There are a number of reasons why Stein posits individual forms. First, as argued in her phenomenological work, our experience shows that each of us has individual potentialities or traits that exist prior to any conscious choices or educational experiences. Before moving to Göttingen to study with Husserl, Stein pursued psychology, studying under William Stern (1871–1938) at the university in Breslau. She was sufficiently impressed and interested in Stern's work to ask him to propose a thesis topic, and she did make one research trip to work on the suggested topic. Although Stein did not finish that project and moved from psychology to phenomenology, her work was influenced by her early studies, especially on the issue of individuality. Stern understood each person as possessing a relatively stable personality core, and, like Stern, Stein emphasizes 'the unfolding or "blooming" of personal qualities out of a core with innate predispositions.'[8]

Stein's early studies provided a motivation for claiming that each of us has an individual form, and the conviction deepened with her study of and experience with spiritual development. One can see an example of this in her elaboration of St Teresa's image of the soul as an interior castle: Stein points out that – like castles – our souls are not fully transparent, not even to ourselves, and they have a character that can be explored and discovered. We are clearly spiritual beings; we are capable of being aware of ourselves, of taking a stance in relation to ourselves, and of being receptive to others. But we also have traits and attributes that we gradually come to know and better understand, and part of spiritual development is the exploration of our souls, a coming to understand our own strengths and weaknesses, motives and tendencies.

Finally, Stein understands our individuality as valuable to God. She says:

> [b]ecause the individual soul blooms in the place prepared for it – made ready through the historical development of its people, its narrower homeland, its family – and because it should be classed according to its pure and full unfolding in the determinate place for it in the eternally unfading garland, therefore, it is not appropriate to understand its essence as a *kind* that can be *individuated* into a multitude of the same structure. [*EeS*, p. 464]

Individuals do not live merely in order to propagate the species, nor are our personalities simply a greater or lesser development of the general human form. Rather, Stein argues that God created unique individuals in order to have in each of us a unique dwelling place.

In the final chapters of *Finite and Eternal Being*, Stein presents a slightly different tripartite understanding of human beings that helps clarify her comments regarding our individual form. She describes us as unities of body (*Leib*), soul (*Seele*), and spirit (*Geist*), echoing biblical language, and distinguishes them: the soul makes the body alive and fashions the material body; the body is that which is shaped by the soul; and the spirit is incorporeal, rational, and free (*EeS*, Chapter 7, §7). Spirit is self-awareness and freedom; it is the center of the person. Unlike human beings, the other animals lack spirit and thus full freedom. They do not have the ability to search out and know themselves, nor can they take a position in regard to both themselves and the exterior world. And therefore other animals are subject to their instincts. In contrast, human beings have freedom both in regard to their bodies and their souls. (Like human beings and unlike the other animals, angels have spirits. Angels, however, do not have souls, that is, there are no hidden depths with which they must acquaint themselves. Humankind therefore stands in a unique spot between the other animals and the angels, with something in common with each.)

Because our individual form lies at the level of soul, Stein in no way denies human freedom. She says, '[t]he human being is a spiritual person because he stands freely opposite not only his body but also his soul [*Seele*], and only so far as he has power over his soul has he also power over his body' (*EeS*, p. 394). We are free because, although having a particularly formed soul, we also have power over our souls, and we may choose which psychological (*seelische*) traits and tendencies to act upon. We can refuse, for example, to entertain envy or we may cut short an aggressive action or thought. Our traits – both bodily and psychological ones – need not dominate our being. We retain an independence and power, albeit not complete, over them. The freedom to choose among options, to negotiate among the possibilities available to us, is central to all personality.

Thus, Stein presents both a tripartite understanding of being and a tripartite understanding of the person. Being is divided into three types and persons are composed of three principles. As there are three principles in the person, there are three expressions of human life that reflect the Trinity: all expressive life originates in our soul (*seelische Sein*), as all divine life flows from the Father; the Son is begotten of the Father, as our living, bodily life is expressive of *seelische* being; and this flowing itself deserves the name of spirit (*EeS*, p. 334). Therefore, all life and being is, she maintains, best understood in sets of three united principles.

Theory of knowledge

Articulating precisely what an essence is and what kind of being it has are central to Stein's project, and she recognizes that a right view of essence is important for challenging modern forms of materialism and defending a Christian morality and worldview. Stein's metaphysical claims have strong similarities to both Scotus's theory of being and his notion of *haecceitas* or individual form, and her understanding of human persons draws heavily from the hylomorphic tradition. Her theory of knowledge, however, is largely phenomenological.[9]

Key to her epistemology is the Husserlian notion of *constitution*. Husserl describes consciousness as intentional: when directed toward something, consciousness intends, or constitutes, what it is directed to *as* some kind of thing. For example, I look out the window and see red, brown, a touch of white, forward motion, etc.; I constitute this combination as a person and not merely as a collection of sensory data. Our experience of the world does not give us a sea of colors but objects that stand out as particular types of things – a flower-box, a cat, buildings, squirrels, and trees.

In order to explain our experience, Husserl distinguishes the sensory data from our intentions. Sensory data is, quite simply, that which we take in through our various senses. In contrast, the intentions are that which we experience the data *as*. Think, for example, of walking into a store and looking at a coat. Initially, you may see the jacket as black, but upon closer inspection, you judge that it is, in fact, midnight blue. The coat's color did not change, but you intended it, first, *as* black and, secondly, *as* midnight blue. The point can be made more clearly with the 'duck–rabbit' picture made famous in Gestalt psychology. The picture can be viewed either *as* a duck or *as* a rabbit. The sensory data itself does not change, but, nonetheless, one views the picture in two different ways, seeing first one structure and then another. Such experiences indicate that the data is distinct from our intentions regarding that data.

Like Husserl, Stein argues that our experience is intentional, and she ties Husserl's claims regarding intentions and intentionality into her claims regarding essences.[10] The intentions through which we structure our experiences are the various essential structures which possess essential being. Because we understand a thing's essential nature (albeit not completely), we can make judgments about our experiences, measuring them against the ideal essence. For example, we might understand the nature of a 'cat' as, among other things, a mammal that moves about on four legs and says 'meow.' When I walk into a room, I might see a four-legged figure in a window, looking particularly relaxed, and take it to be a cat. I thus intend or constitute my sensory experiences as the experience of a cat. It might turn out, however, that upon closer inspection the entity does not meet the specifications of 'cat-ness.' It might not move at all and when touched, might feel more like porcelain than fur. I intended this entity as having the essential structure of 'cat,' but my intentions were not fulfilled, and I began to see it not as a cat but as a statue of a cat.[11]

All knowledge is, Stein claims, made up of such intentions and their fulfillment in experience. And in coming to understand anything, we are constantly making use of essences – even though most of the time, we do this implicitly. We see the world *through* these essential structures yet rarely think about the essential structures themselves. Nonetheless, only because we have an understanding of the essential structure of joy (or any other essence) can we understand some particular experience as a joyful one.

In developing her claims, Stein regularly uses emotional experiences for her examples, and she makes clear throughout her texts that we grasp the world not merely as sensory data but also through our feelings. For example, when she described rationality in her 1916 dissertation, she did not begin with an analysis of 'theoretical acts' (perception, imagination, ideation, or inference); in these theoretical acts, she says, the 'I' may fail to be aware of itself insofar as it becomes absorbed in the object of its acts. In contrast, in *feelings* the 'I' is always present, and our emotions have a direct reference to both the subject and object. This concern for feelings and their philosophical value continues in later writings, and throughout *Finite and Eternal Being* she argues that feelings provide one way of accessing being. For example, in defending her model of the person, she describes a wartime phenomenon: troops marching in ranks through the streets. They appear, to the uninitiated, like an indistinguishable mass, but the mother and fiancée see an individual. Love, Stein says, can feel the mystery of the soldier's unique nature, which cannot be fully grasped intellectually (this ultimately is only known by the omniscient eyes of God) (*EeS*, pp. 464–5).

Thus, Stein appropriates a largely Husserlian epistemology into *Finite and Eternal Being* and, like the phenomenological tradition, she claims that the proper way to approach philosophical questions is to begin with our own experience – including, she insists, our emotional experiences. But in so doing we do not stop at consciousness, ending in idealism; rather, through our experience we have access to being and find structures that we do not construct or create. Thus, Stein moves through epistemology to metaphysics, using the modern 'turn to the subject' as the starting point for her analysis of being. In the Foreword, she says that a strong, but rarely made explicit, influence on her work is Augustine, and we can see an echo of Augustine's inward turn in Stein's work. In the *Confessions*, Augustine argues that we turn upward to God by first turning inward. Likewise, for Stein, properly understanding the real, which is ultimately rooted in God, requires first a proper understanding of self.

Notes

1 For Thomas, form is certainly the principle of being as well as becoming and growth. For Aristotle, form is not the principle of being in the same sense.

2 Stein has several fascinating discussions of matter, and she presents two alternate understandings of matter, an atomic and a dynamic conception. See *EeS*, Chapter 4, esp. §3.

3 *Hylomorphism* comes from the Greek words for matter, *hyle*, and form, *morphe*.

4 Stein dedicates *EeS*, Chapter 3, §12 to a discussion of the Trinity, and her comments are particularly interesting in light of her theory of being.

5   Here I am following Stein's interpretation of *conceptualism.*

6   Stein is not, however, ready to address the question of whether there are individual forms for non-human animals.

7   Stein understands our individuality as arising from many factors – race, generation, family, choices, histories, etc. – not simply our individual form, although that textures all the other elements (see, for example, *EeS*, pp. 406 and 458).

8   Sawicki, 'Editor's Introduction' to *PPH*, p. xiv.

9   In her *Festschrift* essay from 1929, Stein argues that the phenomenological intuition of essence significantly resembles Thomistic abstraction (for example, both affirm that all knowledge begins with sensory experience and both recognize active and passive aspects to the process).

10 I have connected Stein's epistemology with Husserl's, but in its details Stein follows Jean Héring's version more closely. See Héring's 'Bermerkungen über das Wesen, die Wesenheit, und die Idee' in *Jahrbuch für Philosophie und phänomenologische Forschung* 4 (1921): 495–543.

11 Stein makes clear that these intentions are not laid on top of the object, as a scarf is lobbed on top of a coat. In an earlier text, she says: 'The common meaning ... is not loaded on to the object from outside. No logical "treatment" surrounds the object with something essentially foreign to it. Rather, the logical treatment draws the meaning–content from the object's own substance. Meanings reflect back the essential composition of the object' (*PPH*ii, p. 153).

7

Spiritual Writings

A principal translator of Edith Stein's texts, Sr Josephine Koeppel, writes of Stein's Speyer years that, while her lectures were memorable and her teaching excellent, the principal recollections of her were of a woman at prayer.[1] A decade later as a contemplative nun, Stein described the Carmelite life as standing 'before the face of the living God,' and she is often counted among the Christian mystics (*HL*, p. 1). Her texts contain few explicit descriptions of her own interior life; nonetheless, she regularly writes about mystical experiences and has several substantial works focusing on important leaders in mystical theology, especially St Teresa of Avila (1515–82) and St John of the Cross (1542–91). (When she entered the order, Stein chose the name Teresa Benedicta of the Cross: the first name in honor of the leader of the Carmelite reform, Teresa of Avila, and the final in honor of St Teresa's close friend, John of the Cross.)

Stein understands the spiritual life as a path to deeper union with God, and she claims that the core of all mystical experience is 'the person-to-person encounter with God' (*Knowledge and Faith* [*KF*], p. 104). In her commentary on John of the Cross, she notes that visions, revelations, and other supernatural phenomena are inessential to the mystical life and may even be dangerous if they distract us from what is more significant or lead us to fall prey to deceptions. A mystic is not one who experiences such supernatural phenomena, but one who loves the Beloved. The focus, goal, and aim of the mystic – and of all people, whether they are aware of the longing or not – is such a personal encounter and permanent union with the divine. Echoing St Augustine, Stein says, 'God has created human souls for himself. He wants to unite them to himself and to give them even on earth the immeasurable fullness and ineffable bliss of his own divine life' (*SC*, p. 23). In the texts, as she develops this theme, she regularly returns to the significance of inner prayer, the development of a childlike receptivity and the dark nights of the soul, and the redemptive character of suffering. Together these help us to progress toward the goal of our lives, which is the union of our souls with God. Such union requires the work of grace deep within our hearts, purifying our souls; and the path to that purification is the way of the Cross.

Texts

After her conversion to Catholicism, all of Stein's writing and lecturing included, either implicitly or explicitly, religious concerns and questions. We can, however, categorize several texts as primarily spiritual. The most significant of these is Stein's final book (which was left unfinished at her death), *The Science of the Cross* (*Kreuzeswissenschaft*), a commentary on the writings of St John of the Cross. As can be seen by the title that she gave the work, Stein understood John's spiritual writings as offering us a 'science' of spiritual growth. Throughout the book, as Stein leads us through St John's descriptions, moving through the active and passive nights of the soul to the mystical marriage with God, one sees evidence for the argument that there is a structure to the soul and laws according to which to sanctification and purification occur.

Stein approaches her spiritual writings as a phenomenologist and student of human psychology. Her primary concern is a right picture of the workings of the human soul, and she provides numerous illuminating descriptions of spiritual experiences and detailed discussions of, among other things, atheism, faith, and different types of theology.[2] The method is even clearer in a substantial article written just a year prior to her death, 'Ways to Know God,' where she again turns to a spiritual leader (in this article, Dionysius the Areopagite) and focuses on his claims regarding our spiritual development.[3] Fritz Kaufmann, a fellow phenomenologist and friend of Stein's, describes 'Ways to Know God' as 'an interesting and thoroughgoing analysis of the stages of religious experience with the help of phenomenological categories as provided for by the first generation of phenomenologists' (quoted in *KF*, pp. xiv–xv).

In addition to the style, 'Ways to Know God' is noteworthy for its topic. Near the beginning of the essay, Stein points to three related intellectual currents that have formed the Western Christian tradition: Greek thought (especially Aristotle); St Augustine; and 'the legacy of the "Areopagite" ' (*KF*, p. 83). The third is relatively little known, at least in comparison with the first two; nonetheless, 'his effect reaches further than the knowledge about him,' and his thought dominated the Christian intellectual world between the ninth and sixteenth centuries (*KF*, p. 83).

In addition to these two works, Stein wrote a large number of shorter essays and articles, some of which were in honor of various saints or special occasions (for example, Christmas, the feast of St Ambrose, and the founding of the Discalced Carmelites), and she also composed fictive dialogues and poems.[4]

Inner prayer

In the mid nineteenth century, Prosper Guéranger (1805–75) published a twelve-volume text on the liturgical year, initiating what was to be known as the liturgical movement. At the beginning of the twentieth century, Pope Pius X (1835–1914) strengthened the movement with his revision of the breviary, emphasis on frequent communion, and focus on the significance of the mass; and by the 1930s, the liturgical movement was making a significant impact on the life of the German Church, with Stein's early spiritual home at the Benedictine monastery in Beuron as one center. The movement was certainly diverse with a number of quite different advocates and emphases; nonetheless, a few characteristics include: a turn to older patristic and monastic models of worship, a deepening concern for liturgical theology, and a focus on our corporate worship, lived out through a more active and rich understanding of and participation in the mass.

Stein was sympathetic with many of the aims of the liturgical movement. For example, she had a great love of the Eucharist, placing it at the center of her devotional life. After her conversion, she attended daily mass, and throughout her writings and speeches, she recommends turning to the Eucharist for spiritual refreshment.[5] While agreeing with many of the emphases advocated by the liturgical movement, Stein was not, however, unambiguously enthusiastic about all its aspects. She was concerned that too great an emphasis on communal prayer could lead to a de-emphasis of private devotions. Salvation is, after all, *personal* salvation, and the battles between good and evil occur primarily in the heart of each individual.

Stein further argues that separation of the communal and the personal is ultimately a false dichotomy. Rather, she insists that there is an interrelationship between individual, interior prayer and the more public prayers of the service. In a 1936 essay entitled 'The Prayer of the Church,' Stein claims that all prayers – both corporate and private – are Eucharistic. The sacrifice of Christ on the Cross, in mass on the altar, and in glory in heaven are all part of one great thanksgiving in 'gratitude for creation, salvation, and consummation' (*HL*, p. 9). All celebrate one great story. Moreover, all prayer is the prayer of Christ because we, as members of the Church, are members of the Mystical Body of Christ. Therefore, Stein concludes that there is no genuine separation between the private devotion of individuals and corporate worship; one cannot contrast 'subjective' piety and 'objective' public prayer. Rather, '[a]ll authentic prayer is prayer of the Church' (*HL*, p. 15).

Stein questioned at least certain emphases in the liturgical movement and, although not deeply critical, worried about one-sidedness. In her own articulation of our spiritual life, she insists on the importance and interconnection of both the more communal and more private aspects. She opens her essay on the prayer of the Church by turning to the example of Jesus. He made pilgrimages to Jerusalem, participated in the Passover, and regularly shared in the liturgical practices of the synagogue. His religious life, however, was not limited to these public acts. The gospels tell us of His withdrawal from the crowds for prayer and His journeys into the mountains and desert in order to be alone with God.

On the one hand, Stein insists that our spiritual lives are deeply communal and that the spiritual development of each individual is dependent upon her community. She gives the analogy: as a child is given to the care and upbringing of adults throughout its natural development, so too is each person's spiritual development mediated by other human beings. God likes to form people by using others,[6] and 'natural and supernatural factors reveal that even in the life of grace, "it is not good that the man should be alone"' (*EW*, p. 127).

Further, Stein sees in each individual life, an echo of the whole. She says, 'the great events of the cosmic drama concerning the fall of man and redemption are renewed again and again in the life of the Church and in each human soul' (*EW*, pp. 125–6). Our lives have a cosmic significance, and the great events of the Christian story are also the events of each life:

[e]ach individual has his place and task in the one great development of humanity. Humanity is to be understood as one great individual; it is possible to understand salvation history only by this interpretation. Each person is a member of this whole, and the essential structure of the whole is shown in every member; but, at the same time, each has his own character as a member which he must develop if the whole is to attain development. The species *humanity* is realized perfectly only in the course of world history in which the great individual, humanity, becomes concrete. (*EW*, p. 189)

The individual and communal are related, and loving another rightly requires the recognition not merely that I should be sympathetic to another's plight, but also, more importantly, that I am in solidarity with the other, that we are all part of one Body.

On the other hand, however, Stein refuses to compromise the deeply private and personal aspects of spiritual development. In *The Science of the Cross* and in a number of her philosophical writings,[7] she uses spatial images for the soul, often employing St Teresa of Avila's image of an interior castle. Our souls are like a dwelling with many rooms, some are near the outer wall and others more deeply inside. Many of the rooms are hidden, even from ourselves. The I or ego lives within the soul, moving among the different rooms and layers. Most of the time, it lives in the more exterior rooms. Things outside ourselves – our duties, tasks, possessions, and sensory preoccupations – often absorb us and distract us from our interior, preventing the I from inhabiting its most interior spaces, and in our fallenness, we disperse ourselves in external things. We are, however, most at home, most fully ourselves, in the more interior rooms. Thus, our task is gradually to win possession of our own souls.

Stein claims that what we see, both in ourselves and in others, both the faults and virtues, is only the surface of the soul. That out of which the expressions come is largely hidden, seen clearly and fully only by God. In a letter to a friend, she says:

what we believe we understand about our own soul is, after all, only a fleeting reflection of what will remain God's secret until the day all will be made manifest. My great joy consists in the hope of that future clarity. Faith in the secret history must always strengthen us when what we actually perceive (about ourselves or about others) might discourage us. (*Letters*, no. 320)

God's grace works in that deep interior, changing the person in ways often unknown even to the person herself. In her writings on the saints, Stein emphasizes that in secrecy, the Lord forms a soul; deep in our hearts, God's grace effects change, transforming us more and more into His likeness. The divine ray is '[s]een by no human eye,' but lovingly forms the living building-blocks which are 'brought together into a church first of all invisible' (*HL*, p. 109). Gradually, the results of God's grace working in our interior bloom forth, and God's hidden work shows itself in the fruits of the Spirit. It is in the 'mysterious depths' of the soul that the work of salvation occurs, in 'obscurity and stillness' (*HL*, pp. 12 and 15). In 'concealment and silence,' the divine plan is unfolded, and '[i]n the silent dialogue with their Lord of souls consecrated to God, the events of Church history are prepared that, visible far and wide, renew the face of the earth' (*HL*, pp. 12 and 13).

In a poem (written most likely in 1938 as she was leaving the monastery in Cologne), Stein writes:

The Eternal who made all creatures,
Who, thrice holy, encompasses all being,
In addition has a silent, special kingdom of his own.

The innermost chamber of the human soul
Is the Trinity's favorite place to be,
His heavenly throne on earth. (*HL*, p. 135)

We are most fully ourselves in this most interior realm, and we meet God in the innermost room of our souls. Like Augustine and John of the Cross, Stein understands the ascent to God as a journey into the soul: we are drawn upward by turning inward (*SC*, p. 116). In a poem from 1942, she states even more powerfully:

You, nearer to me than I to myself
And more interior than my most interior
And still impalpable and intangible
And beyond any name: Holy Spirit –
Eternal love! (*HL*, p. 141)

Stein likes to say that in genuinely meeting God, one is 'seized in his innermost being' (*KF*, p. 105). It is from such a touch that we come both to self-understanding and to an understanding of God.

122

Stein does not see this inward turn as a withdrawal from the world. It is, rather, the development of a right relationship and a true vision of the world; she understands it not as detachment from, but as true love of creation. (Stein interestingly notes in *Die Seelenburg* [*The Castle of the Soul*] that 'no one has so entered the depths of the soul as the human beings who have grasped the world with a hot heart and then loosened the entanglement through the strong hand of God and were pulled into the proper interior and the innermost.'[8] She suggests here that a great initial love of this world can be a help in spiritual development: one who first sees the beauty of this world and then has his eyes turned to an even greater beauty, has more rightly recognized the value of heaven than someone who begins by feeling indifferent to this world. The incomparable greatness of the heavenly is likely to strike less forcefully him who is little awed by the earthly.)

As we move more deeply into our souls, developing a more intimate union with God, we gain increasing access to the real – we understand ourselves and others more fully – and thus we also gain increasing freedom. Stein claims that the center point of the soul is where one hears the voice of conscience and where truly free personal decisions are made. Any decision made from a more external point is, in a real sense, superficial because, it is only when one has the most profound point of view that one is 'capable of judging all things by their ultimate standards' (*SC*, p.120). Other decisions are a kind of blind choice. The person does not know the full value either of what she has chosen or of what she has given up. Only by moving into the deeper realms of the soul does she gain a purer, more appropriate view of and attitude toward the world.[9]

Thus, Stein claims that a genuine relationship with the world is only possible from such a deep point, and the deeper one moves into her own interior, the more authentically one relates to the world. She insists strongly that such understanding, relating, and loving of the earthly is a central part of the task to which we have been called. In a short, but eloquent essay on the meaning of Christmas, she says that 'our love for our fellow human beings is the measure of our love for God.'[10] In turning inward to find God, we are directed outward toward others.

Yet, ironically, the deeper one enters into one's own soul, the less activity she does. Our freedom lies ultimately in our receptivity, not our activity. In a discussion of prayer, Stein repeats the point that highest human achievement is to be receptive and the deepest prayer is one in which 'the soul is no longer active by virtue of its own efforts, but is simply a receptacle for grace' (*HL*, p. 38). The highest state is not a discursive one, but, as Stein said in her early phenomenological works, 'a state of resting in God' (*PPH*i, p. 84).

No created being can by itself enter this interior; without divine assistance, we cannot even know our own soul. Therefore, a full understanding and transformation of the soul occurs not through the force of the will, but only through grace. Stein does, however, make practical suggestions for how one can help open herself to grace. While ultimately union with God occurs through grace and not through our efforts, we are still free and thus can cooperate or refuse to cooperate with God, and some actions can better put us in a place to receive God's work in us. In essays written while she was teaching, Stein notes that often we are distracted, filled with worries about how to complete tasks and fulfill the duties of the day, or frustrated by a million interruptions and little problems. And in a short essay on inner stillness, she says, '[w]e cannot achieve in each hour what we want, perhaps in none. We must contend with our own fatigue, unforeseen interruptions, shortcomings of the children, diverse vexations, indignities, anxieties' (*EW*, p. 144). At nightfall, we see that 'everything was patchwork and much which one had planned left undone,' little actions or omissions cause shame and regret, and the worry of the day wears us down. In that state, we should 'take all as it is, lay it in God's hands, and offer it up to Him' (*EW*, p. 145). Stein calls us to quiet our souls, to go to God's altar. In daily communion before the tabernacle, we learn to forget the self, becoming 'free of all one's own wishes and pretensions' and gaining 'a heart open to all the needs and wants of others' (*EW*, p. 56). It is there that we are transformed, and become receptive to God's work in us. We are then able to recognize what our true duties are and see things from a divine perspective, and there our hearts are once again inflamed to love.

Receptivity and the Dark Night of the Soul

Stein began her commentary on St John of the Cross at the request of her superiors on the occasion of the fourth centenary celebration of the saint's birth, and her introduction to the text develops many ideas already present in her phenomenological works. For example, she points to inappropriate responses to value – that is, failures to have right emotional responses to the value of the things. The emotional dullness characteristic of our fallen state, and plaguing us until we are perfected, is particularly painful in the religious sphere. Stein notes that '[m]any Christians feel depressed because the events of the Gospel do not – or do no longer – impress them as they ought and fail to affect and shape their lives' (*SC*, p. 2). Growing in sanctity includes developing right emotional responses, and the rebirth of the soul includes the development of a childlike receptivity (for we are to become as children). We should respond joyfully to that which is joyful, with sadness to that which is sad, and in awe before that which is awesome. Each heart should be filled with 'a living, moving power joyfully ready to let itself be formed, unhampered by false inhibitions and rigidity' (*SC*, p. 2).

Stein's opening comments shape her presentation of John of the Cross's dark night of the soul and path to the mystical marriage of the soul to God. Throughout her commentary she is concerned with our transformations of heart, understanding with St John that full conversion requires that we traverse through many nights. A number of these can be clearly distinguished. First, one can differentiate the active dark night of the soul (which Stein draws from *Ascent of Mount Carmel*) from the passive dark night (drawn from *Dark Night of the Soul*). The active night involves our efforts to free ourselves from our sensuous nature. In contrast, the passive night is God's work preventing us from hindering our own progress and Himself perfecting our souls. Both are needed because, as Stein says, a person 'can surrender himself to crucifixion, but he cannot crucify himself. Hence what has been begun in the active Night must be perfected by the passive Night, that is, by God himself' (*SC*, p. 33).

Secondly, St John distinguishes the night of the senses, of reason, and of memory. Before we enter the 'darkness,' we feel largely at home in the world, enjoying its pleasures and loving its comforts. In order to long for comforts not of this world and to take pleasure in truer goods, one must first turn his heart away from the love of this world. Thus, John calls us to renounce the enjoyment of the senses. (Ironically, however, only in the renunciation of earthly things can one rightly enjoy them. Stein says: 'the joy in creatures is increased by renouncing them; it is a joy that the greedy man can never taste, because in his unrest he lacks the necessary freedom of spirit. The man who is free from possessions sees their true natural and supernatural worth' [*SC*, p. 68].)

One seeks God – not the pleasant or the comfortable, not even the pleasant or comfortable in the spiritual realm (peace in prayer, sweetness, etc.) – but God Himself. As one enters the dark night, even spiritual exercises become arid and dry, more of a torment than a comfort. Nothing interests the soul; it simply wants to rest. Thus,

Stein suggests that the image of night is appropriate: it is like the fall of night where the cares of the world disappear, darkness falls on the senses, and the terrors of the night haunt.[11]

Likewise, darkness falls upon natural reason. Because our natural reasoning powers are incapable of fully grasping the divine, they too must be darkened.[12] One goes forward in the dark light of faith, accepting what is presented without being able clearly to grasp it by one's own reason and insight:

> [i]f one speaks to a man of something he has never seen, and if he knows nothing similar that could help him, he will indeed be able to grasp the name but will never form an idea of the thing, as a man born blind does not know what colour is. We are in a similar condition with regard to faith. It tells us of things we have never heard or seen; nor do we know anything resembling them. We can accept what we are told only by eliminating the light of our natural knowledge. We must consent to what we hear without its being introduced to us by one of our senses. Hence faith is a completely dark night to the soul. But for this very reason it gives it light: a knowledge of absolute certainty surpassing every other knowledge and science, so that only perfect contemplation will produce the right conception of faith. (SC, pp. 39–40)

Stein is not advocating fideism.[13] In the light of faith, one rises above the natural activity of reason but is not detached from reason; '[r]ather, in the new world opened up by faith the natural powers of the mind are given a wealth of fresh material on which to act' (SC, p. 85).

She expands on this by claiming that faith is the turning, not to particular truths that the Christian faith announces, but to the person announced, to God Himself. Faith reveals not something incomprehensible, but 'the Incomprehensible One who contains the essence of all truths of faith yet transcends them all in his very Incomprehensibility, in darkness and indistinction' (SC, p. 100). Faith, as Stein understands it, should not be opposed to reason, but to distrust. She goes on to insist that faith is 'the firm conviction that God exists, the belief that all he has revealed is true, and a loving readiness to be guided by the divine will' (SC, p. 127); the emphasis should be on the final claim about our posture of heart. In a lecture from a number of years earlier, she says of faith that it is neither a fancy of one's imagination nor a pious emotion, but, 'on the contrary, it is an intellectual recognition (if not a rational permeation) and a voluntary acceptance by the will; a complete development of faith is one of the most profound acts of the individual, one in which all his powers become acute' (*EW*, p. 244).

Stein meditated on John of the Cross's spiritual writings during a number of retreats, and in a long letter written just before she began her commentary, she summarizes many of the themes developed more fully in her book and endorses St John's understanding of spiritual development. To the question of whether we should strive for perfect love, she responds, '[f]or this we were created.' And in response to the question of how we might achieve this, she advises, following St John:

> Try with all our might to be empty: the senses mortified; the memory as free as possible from all images of this world and, through hope, directed toward heaven; the understanding stripped of natural seeking and ruminating, directed to God in the straightforward gaze of faith; the will ... surrendered to God in love. (*Letters*, no. 311)

And in *The Science of the Cross*, she accounts for the difficulty of this task: 'because God is deep and infinite, their [our understanding's, will's, and memory's] capacity, too, is in a certain sense infinite, their thirst and hunger are infinite, the process of their destruction and their pain are an unending death' (p. 156).

The images used by both John of the Cross and Edith Stein are stark: the process is like death, requiring the mortification of the senses, memory, and understanding; it is like a fire consuming us. Despite the images, this darkness of soul is actually not a night but, rather, a great brightness. It is the night and 'death' of the senses and of natural reason precisely because it is a radiance too bright for their powers; it throws them in darkness as the eyes are thrown in darkness upon entering the sunlight after a passage through a cave. The senses, memory, and understanding are put in pain because they must turn from what they are used to, from the less to the more perfect. Before the soul saw only in its own darkness; it was attuned only to its own imperfections. But when transformed by the Light, it begins to see its own blackness for what it is and, then gradually, the beauty of the Light itself:

> [f]ormerly the flame was a terror to the will, because it made it painfully aware of its own hardness and aridity. The will could not sense the delicacy and loveliness of the flame, nor could it taste its

127

sweetness, because its taste had been spoiled by perverse inclinations. The soul was incapable of grasping the infinite treasures and delights of the flame of love under whose influence it only realized its own poverty and misery. (SC, p. 144)

Through the night, the soul is transformed to respond rightly to the heavenly light, and the darkness of the night is precisely the adjustment to a far greater Light.

Suffering

While much of *The Science of the Cross* focuses on the Dark Night of the Soul, a major theme in many of Stein's spiritual writings is the Cross itself. God has chosen that redemption come through suffering. It is not suffering simply for the sake of suffering; as Stein notes, '[t]he Cross is not an end in itself.' Nonetheless: 'it is not only a sign, it is the strong weapon of Christ, the shepherd's staff with which the divine David fights against the infernal Goliath, which he knocks at the gate of heaven and opens it. Then the divine light streams out, embracing all those who follow the crucified Lord' (*SC*, pp. 10–11). Redemption, that is, union with God, is the goal; however, God chose to use the Cross as the instrument for our salvation.

Jesus is our example and guide in all our suffering, for, Stein argues, He alone experienced the most excruciating of pain, to be abandoned by God; He alone could experience such pain. Jesus is both divine and human, and in that union lies the mystery of our salvation:

for as God he could not have suffered, and as a mere man he could not have grasped the good of which he deprived himself. Thus the Incarnation is the condition of this suffering; and Christ's human nature is the instrument of Redemption because it is both capable of suffering and actually suffered. (*SC*, p. 194)

Christ as Incarnate was the only one who could truly suffer the ultimate pain – to be severed from God. In the Garden, He accepted that fate; on the Cross, He suffered that fate. All our suffering may approximate that, but it can only approximate and participate in a limited way in His experience. We cannot, however, know the depth of His pain, for that very pain has saved us from that fate.

Nevertheless, the burdens, pain, and suffering of this life can lead us to identify more fully with Christ, learning to walk more closely with him, even and especially in His suffering. Stein strongly calls us to imitate Christ, and, she says, for all 'chosen to attend the marriage supper of the Lamb,' that imitation includes walking the road to Golgotha (*HL*, p. 99). Christ has planted the seeds of our salvation, but they must take root and grow. That growth (that is, the working out of our salvation) requires that each of us take up our cross and follow in His path. Stein understands each of our individual stories as a re-enactment of the divine drama, and in becoming more like Christ, we allow ourselves to be formed 'into the image of him who bore the Cross and died on it' (*SC*, p. 4).

Suffering can be sanctifying; it is part of the battle against our corrupted nature and part of our conversion into the full image of Christ. In addition, Stein also claims that our suffering can – under certain circumstances – be expiatious for others. She notes that the battle against evil is not fully won; '[t]he world is still deluged by mire' and only a few have fully escaped the clutches of sin (*HL*, p. 91). Those following Christ in this battle against corrupted human nature have the Cross as their chief weapon, and the meaning of the Cross is the victory over the burden of our own corruption. Echoing the biblical claims regarding propitiation, she claims that the restoration of our nature is a free gift lovingly given by the Father, but, nonetheless, 'this may not occur at the expense of divine holiness and justice. The entire sum of human failures from the first Fall up to the Day of Judgment must be blotted out by a corresponding measure of expiation [*Sühneleistungen*]. The way of the cross is this expiation [*Sühne*]' (*HL*, pp. 91–2).

Stein goes on to argue that we may participate in Christ's work by bearing a burden 'in remembrance of the suffering Savior,' and in freely accepting suffering, one has 'canceled some of the mighty load of human sin and has helped the Lord carry his burden' (*HL*, p. 92). She gives a memorable image for her claim, suggesting that the prospect of those who would help carry the burden strengthened Jesus in His walk to Golgotha and helped Him up when He fell. Such voluntary expiatory suffering is 'not merely a pious reminder of the suffering of the Lord,' but truly unites one to Jesus and can be a cooperation with him in the work of salvation (*HL*, p. 92).[14] She says in a letter:

[t]here is a vocation to suffer with Christ and thereby to cooperate with him in his work of salvation. When we are united with the

Lord, we are members of the mystical body of Christ: Christ lives on in his members and continues to suffer in them. And the suffering borne in union with the Lord is his suffering, incorporated in the great work of salvation and fruitful therein. That is a fundamental premise of all religious life, above all of the life of Carmel, to stand proxy for sinners through voluntary and joyous suffering, and to cooperate in the salvation of humankind. (*Letters*, no. 129)

Suffering accepted willingly and 'carried to the end' is, she says, 'reckoned before God as a true martyrdom' (*Letters*, no. 302). And in willingly suffering for others, we give proof of our love of God (see *HL*, p. 73).

Stein has a strong conviction of the unity of all believers in the Mystical Body of Christ. This theme shows up repeatedly in all of her post-conversion writings, and only in the light of her firm belief in our fundamental unity do her claims regarding the potentially expiatory character of suffering make sense. She insists that those with the desire to participate in the sufferings of Christ 'by no means deny that Good Friday is past and that the work of salvation has been accomplished' (*HL*, p. 93). Only those who are already saved,

only children of grace, can in fact be bearers of Christ's cross. Only in union with the divine Head does human suffering take on expiatory power. To suffer and to be happy although suffering, to have one's feet on the earth, to walk on the dirty and rough paths of this earth and yet to be enthroned with Christ at the Father's right hand, to laugh and cry with the children of this world and ceaselessly sing the praises of God with the choirs of angels – this is the life of the Christian until the morning of eternity breaks forth. (*HL*, p. 93)

If one understands human beings in an atomistic way, as isolated individuals, her claims will be unintelligible. She is convinced that the image of the Body is not merely a metaphor but, rather, reveals an important truth. The willingness to walk the path of Christ and to be united with Him requires that one, Stein claims, also be willing to suffer as He did. She does not mean that one should be willing to suffer in a way somewhat analogous to Him, but to suffer *with* Him, carrying His burden, walking His path, and allowing His life to flow through us.

Stein is careful to distinguish the desire to participate in the expiatory suffering of Christ from a masochistic desire for pain.

The latter is a sensory longing, one contrary to nature and thus perverse. It is quite the opposite of a right spiritual desire to be more fully united with Christ and to participate in His work in the world. She says, '[o]nly someone whose spiritual eyes have been opened to the supernatural correlations of worldly events can desire suffering in expiation, and this is only possible for people in whom the spirit of Christ dwells' (*HL*, p. 92). It requires a great love of both Christ and the world to desire to suffer with Christ, and only someone in whom the spirit of Christ lives and who is given the grace and power of God can so desire. (In her last will and testament, Stein indicates such a desire, offering her own future sufferings for others.)

Stein understands sanctification as a *science* or *art* of the Cross, and she makes clear that we are not made perfect through our own efforts. We may cooperate with grace, but all genuine sanctification is the work of God. Our task lies primarily in 'getting out of the way' of God's work within us. As Stein says in a letter, '[i]f one is intent on having all of one's life consist exclusively of sacrifices, the danger of pharisaism is around the corner' (*Letters*, no. 94). To *look* for sufferings and mortifications, in contrast to *accepting* those which are given, is an assertion of our own will rather than a submission to the divine will. One then runs the risk of self-righteous hypocrisy and misses the real point of all suffering: a deeper relationship and unification with God. In *The Science of the Cross*, she says, '[t]he Cross laid upon a man by God, whether it be external or interior, is more effective than mortification practised from one's own choice' (*SC*, p. 227). For all mortifications chosen are our own, and in them, we still strive to serve our own will.

All suffering – in imitation of Christ, for purification, or for expiation – has as its goal union with God.[15] The key to such union is obedience. The will of the person and the will of God become one, and genuine obedience requires that the person determines to deny her own will and follow God's. Stein warns, '[e]very aversion, any anger and resentment we tolerate in our hearts, closes the door to the Savior' (*HL*, p. 101). Rather, in denying our own will, desires, and inclinations, we are more deeply united to the one who was obedient unto death.

In a 1930 lecture, Stein describes the religious vocation as one of 'total surrender of the whole person and his or her entire life to the service of God,' and her continual theme in nearly all her lectures is a call for us to learn to live at the hand of the Lord (see *Letters*, no. 89 and *EW*, p. 52). The greatest obstacles to this are not external, but internal. Stein makes the strong statement that the Savior 'has spilled his heart's blood to win your heart. If you want to follow him in holy *purity*, your heart must be free of every earthly desire. Jesus, the Crucified, is to be the only object of your longings, your wishes, your thoughts' (*HL*, p. 95).

Despite the strong language, such a union does not require the destruction of the person, her will, or her knowledge but, rather, with her full consent, she receives God into herself. Stein regularly cites the principle that grace perfects nature, it does not destroy it (*gratia perficit naturam, non destruit*). While grace helps us to transcend our natural limitations, this 'can never be attained by an arbitrary battle against nature and by denial of natural limitations but only through humble submission to the God-given order' (EW, p. 85). The language of denial, death of self, and utter submission articulate what our corrupted nature must undergo, but that death leads to the freedom and full release of the self as she was intended by God. Freedom is often thought of as freedom from another's will, doing what I want to do, and in order to achieve this, we 'engage in bloody battles and sacrifice life and limb' (*HL*, p. 100). But true freedom lies not in freedom from external restrictions, but in the freedom to follow the Spirit of God. God demands our obedience because the human will is blind and weak; He demands our poverty 'because hands must be empty of earth's goods to receive the goods of heaven' (*HL*, p. 95); and He longs for our life because He wishes to give us His own. At the highest stage, when the soul has been perfected and passionately and rightly loves God, it can finally receive God and thus be truly with Him. And, she says, '[t]he day on which God has unrestricted power over our hearts we shall also have unrestricted power over his' (*HL*, p. 101). She ends an essay on St Elizabeth of Hungary with Augustine's words, '*Ama et fac quod vis*' – love and do what you will (*HL*, p. 28). When we reach the highest stage, in the mystical marriage, there may finally be the 'voluntary mutual surrender of God and the soul,' the full communion our hearts have so deeply longed for (*SC*, p. 122).

Notes

1 Koeppel writes of Stein's Speyer years, '[t]he woman kneeling for hours on a prie-dieu in a corner near the sanctuary of St Magdalena's, or at a kneeler in Beuron's Benedictine Arch-abbey, a silent person even known on rare occasions to make an all-night vigil in a convent chapel without tiring, this is the Edith Stein whom observers recalled' (*Edith Stein: Philosopher and Mystic*, p. 75).

2   Her method, however, may also be the weakness of her work. Several commentators, including Hilda Graef, who first translated *The Science of the Cross* into English, argue that Stein's formation did not appropriately prepare her for the study of mystical theology. See Graef's *The Scholar and the Cross: The Life and Works of Edith Stein* (Westminster, MD: Newman Press, 1995; New York: Longmans, Green, 1955), esp. Chapter 22.

3   'Ways to Know God' was composed between 1940 and 1941 and originally intended for the then newly established American periodical *Journal of Philosophy and Phenomenological Research*. Stein's article was not published in this journal, however, but appeared instead in *The Thomist*. Ironically, although written for a US audience, the article was published first – by just a few months – in a Dutch journal.

4   Many of these have been collected in *The Hidden Life*. See also Susanne Batzdorff (ed.), *Edith Stein: Selected Writings* and John Sullivan (ed.), *Edith Stein: Essential Writings*.

5   She acknowledges that different devotional practices – for example, contemplation, spiritual reading, and participation in more popular services – are fruitful in different ways for various people. Each person should find ways 'suitable for bringing about union with the eternal, keeping it alive or also enlivening it anew' (*EW*, p. 145).

6   Similarly, in her commentary on St John of the Cross, she quotes St John's comment that 'God desires particularly that men should be guided by other men' (*SC*, p. 49).

7   See especially *EeS*, Chapter 7, and *Die Seelenburg*, the appendix on Teresa of Avila.

8   *Welt und Person*, *ESW* VI, p. 66.

9   Ibid., p. 62

10 *Ganzheitliches Leben*, *ESW* XII, p. 201. Koeppel has translated a significant portion of the essay in *Edith Stein*, and I am following her translation (p. 18).

11 One must distinguish the Dark Night proper from sinfulness. In both cases one may lose interest in spiritual exercises; in the Dark Night, however, one 'always desires to serve God' (*SC*, p. 34).

12 In 'Ways to Know God,' Stein claims that the purpose of image-language is 'to conceal what is holy from the profaning images of the throng and to unveil it for those who are striving for holiness' (*KF*, p. 90).

13 In a letter from 1938, she writes: '[a]ll who seek truth seek God, whether this is clear to them or not' (*Letters*, no. 272), and in *Science of the Cross*, she says: '[t]he seeker after truth lives predominantly in the sphere of rational research; if he is really concerned with truth itself, not only with amassing particular kinds of knowledge, he is probably nearer to God, who is Truth, than he himself realizes' (p. 122).

14 Stein repeats this theme, saying of Elijah: '[b]y living penitentially, he atones [*sühnt*] for the sins of his time' (HL, p. 2).

15 Stein distinguishes three ways to understand union with God. First, there is the substantial union God has with all things through which he keeps them in being. Secondly, there is 'the indwelling of grace in the soul' (*SC*, p. 125). And, finally, there is the mystical marriage, 'the transforming, divinizing union through perfect love' (SC, p. 125). The first is common to all creatures and involves a one-sided relation of dependence of the creature on the Creator. The second, while possible only for spiritual–personal beings (because it requires the free acceptance of the grace), is not the complete union. God works in all souls open to Him, perfecting them and creating an abode for Himself within them. Only in the final case does God have a true home within the soul.

8

Edith Stein since her Death: The Jewish–Catholic Dialogue

In the final chapter, I would like to discuss something which concerns less Stein's life or writings and more the controversies that arose surrounding her beatification and canonization. In 1983 Joseph Cardinal Höffner signed a petition requesting that Stein be considered a martyr, and in 1987 she was beatified both because of her heroic virtue and because of her martyrdom. The declaration of Stein as a martyr enabled her beatification and canonization to move rather quickly. (In order to be canonized, a person must have three miracles attributed to him or her, except in the case of martyrs, who need only one miracle for canonization and none for beatification.) But that declaration also opened up rather painful questions, and the resulting debates have focused on the legitimacy of calling Stein a martyr, the Catholic Church's understanding of the Holocaust (or the Shoah), the purpose of canonizing a prominent Jewish convert, and Catholic–Jewish relations. None of the issues are simple, but looking, albeit cursorily, at the debates may indicate why the name Edith Stein stands at the center of several difficult questions for both Christianity and Judaism.

It is clear that Stein is not a martyr in the classic sense; she did not stand defending the faith in a literal lion's den or before a firing squad. She died, most likely, in a chamber amid Jewish Catholics.[1] She was chosen by the Nazi leaders, in large part, because of her heritage and bloodlines. Therefore, it appears that she died because she was a Jew.

The decision to kill Stein, as well as the 300 other Catholics of Jewish descent rounded up on the same transport, was, however, clearly in direct response to the actions of the Catholic bishops standing up against injustice and hatred. Prior to the bishops' decision to read a pastoral letter condemning the practices of the National Socialists in the Netherlands, converted Jews were exempt from deportation. Therefore, Stein died in and amid actions defending the faith, although she had not, by her personal actions or words, provoked the Nazis. (That she was in agreement with the bishops' actions can be ascertained from her own continual criticism of National Socialism, her insistence on saying 'Praised be Christ Jesus' rather than *'Heil Hitler'* before Nazi administrators, and her appeal to the Pope to write an encyclical denouncing the policies of National Socialism.)

The relator of Stein's cause, Fr Ambrogio Eszer, points to the Nazis as modern tyrants, who, though stating that they were not against the Christian religion, proved through their very actions and ideology to be deeply anti-Christian. Such 'modern tyrants' – although professing not to care about the religious beliefs of their victims – nonetheless do attack the faith. Persecution occurs not only in direct attacks on the doctrines of Christianity, but also in more 'indirect' attacks which undermine the faith. As tyrants in our era differ from those of previous times, so, Eszer argues, should our understanding of what it means to stand up to religious persecution and what it means to be a martyr for the faith.[2]

But the Catholic case for Stein's martyrdom is not based solely on the events of 1942. In her last will and testament from 1939, Stein clearly expresses her willingness to suffer for the faith, and in the conclusion to that document, she says:

> I joyfully accept in advance the death God has appointed for me, in perfect submission to his most holy will. May the Lord accept my life and death for the honor and glory of his name, for the needs of his holy Church – especially for the preservation, sanctification, and final perfecting of our holy Order, and in particular for the Carmels of Cologne and Echt – for the Jewish people, that the Lord may be received by his own and his Kingdom come in glory, for the deliverance of Germany and peace throughout the world, and finally, for all my relatives living and dead and all whom God has given me: may none of them be lost.[3]

As seen in the previous chapter, Stein saw suffering as, potentially, participating in Jesus's expiatory work, and here she offers herself for that purpose. The events of 1933 and afterwards show that Stein was well aware of the impending dangers and, rather than asking for mercy, she asked that what she suffers may be redemptive. Thus, the case for her martyrdom rests both on the events surrounding her arrest and execution and her own explicit willingness to suffer death for the sake of the faith.

The questions raised do not, however, simply concern the legitimacy of calling Stein a martyr, but also include concerns regarding the Catholic Church's understanding of the Shoah. Stein was beatified on May 1, 1987, just as a house of Carmelite nuns was planning to build a monastery outside the gates of Auschwitz[4] (a similar monastery has been built overlooking Dachau) and the Pope was extending an invitation to the Austrian president, Kurt Waldheim, who had recently been accused of involvement in Nazi atrocities in Yugoslavia during the Second World War.[5] The combination of these decisions raised questions in the Jewish community about how the Catholic Church understands the Shoah. Declaring a Catholic nun a Holocaust martyr (and thereby showing that the Catholic Church suffered a 'blood witness to the crimes and horrors of the Nazis')[6], establishing a Christian center of prayer at the site of such horror, and welcoming one of the alleged perpetrators of the crimes into a place of great honor all seem to imply a Christian appropriation of the events. The Catholic Church put forward one of its own as a martyr of the events, placed one of its own sites of prayer at the gates of the most famous concentration camp, and welcomed – offering forgiveness and acceptance? – one of the criminals to speak with the leader of the Church. The question then arose: as the primary victims of the 'Final Solution,' should not the Jews rather than the Catholics claim the martyrs and make the overtures for whatever redemption is possible?

Daniel Polish admits that 'claiming' the Shoah may seem rather out of place. Who wants to claim such a horror? But he goes on to say that it has significance for the Jewish community. Jewish identity lies not in their ability to trace their lineage to a king or deity, but in their lineage as descendants of runaway slaves, and likewise

> With all of its pain the holocaust has become a *sanctum* for us. It reminds us of our continuing special relationship with God. We remain an instrument of His purpose in the ongoing work of shaping human destiny. It has become a rallying-point for our collective experience, a key to our shared identity. Jews are Jews

because we share that anguish. Jews are Jews because we recognize one another as similarly traumatized by that horror.[7]

The fear of the Jewish community is that in honoring Stein, the Church has made precisely such a move, taking the *sanctum* of the Shoah away from the Jewish community and appropriating it as its own symbol and part of Christ's redemptive work. The Christian Church has always had the ability to adapt itself to different cultural and religious climates. In its claim that all that is, is the Lord's, Christianity has found Jesus's print everywhere. The Church is able to assimilate itself to all kinds of situations and cultures; this is much of the key to its success. And it is precisely this success that leads the Jewish community to be suspicious of the elevation of Edith Stein as a Holocaust martyr.

One could further add the way in which anti-Semitism – which was, prior to Vatican II, far too rarely condemned by the Church and often encouraged – played into the ease with which Nazi policies were put into action. And the Nazis themselves were, for the most part, Christians, even if nominal ones. The fear then arises that the Catholic Church, in honoring Stein as a martyr, is failing to recognize the explicit anti-Semitism of the Nazi policies and may be failing to recognize its own complicity in the events by honoring one of 'its own' victims.

The hope of the Church is clearly that in honoring Stein, it will call to mind the Shoah, not letting the suffering and great evils committed be forgotten. In his canonization speech, Pope John Paul II insists that in celebrating Stein, we must also remember the Shoah, 'that cruel plan to exterminate a people, a plan to which millions of our Jewish brothers and sisters fell victim.'[8] Far from forgetting the Jewish victims of the Second World War, those who honor Stein should, instead, remember those victims and learn to be more vigilant in preventing any such event from occurring again. This is a goal that both the Jewish and Catholic communities agree to be vital, but the key concern for the former, however, is that the event be remembered as it ought to be.

Finally, and most broadly, the events raise the question of what implications follow from the declaration of Stein as a saint for relations between the Catholic and Jewish communities. (The recent elevation of Stein includes not only her canonization, but also the prominence Pope John Paul II gave to Stein in citing her importance as a thinker in his 1998 encyclical *Fides et Ratio* and his 1999 pronouncement of Stein as co-patroness of Europe.) Relations between the two religious communities have always been tense. Both accept the same sacred writings (what the Christian community has termed the Old Testament); both recognize the significance of the call of Abraham, the Exodus, the anointing of David, and the prophecies of the Messiah. But the Christian community has interpreted those Scriptures in the light of Jesus, arguing for a New Testament and a New Covenant. It is little surprise that there are tensions. Added to these inherent tensions are the history of explicit and implicit anti-Semitism on the part of Christians and the centuries of pressure, in more and less direct forms, for Jewish assimilation in the Christian West.

A number of passages in Stein's autobiography reveal that she was affected by these pressures; there seems to be a lack of understanding of the Jewish tradition, a misunderstanding of many of the legal and dietary restrictions, and a prejudice against Eastern Jews. It is, ironically, after her conversion to Catholicism that Stein identifies herself most strongly with the Jewish people, taking pride in her heritage and regularly insisting on her own Jewishness. Although her family understood her conversion and especially her entrance into a Carmelite monastery as a separation and rejection of her identity as a Jew, Stein herself saw it otherwise. In a letter from October 31, 1938, she writes,

> I trust that, from eternity, Mother will take care of them [her family]. And in the Lord's having accepted my life for all of them. I keep having to think of Queen Esther who was taken from among her people precisely so that she might represent them before the king. I am a very poor and powerless little Esther, but the King who chose me is infinitely great and merciful.

Since Vatican II, the Church has been actively attempting to forge a new relationship with Judaism, backing away from claims that imply God's covenant with the Jews is invalid or those that would encourage the mass conversion of Jews. Thus, the canonization of a prominent Jewish convert may appear ill-timed at best. Freda Mary Oben, however, makes the argument that Stein is, in fact, an 'ecumenical' figure.[9] First, Oben points out that Stein was not at the time of her conversion, nor had she been for more than a decade before, a practicing Jew. She had little theological training and could be described as an agnostic or atheist in the years prior to her conversion. Thus, she did not move from deep Jewish beliefs and practices to Christian ones, but rather her path led her from an agnostic culturally assimilated Jew to a believing Catholic Christian. Secondly, Stein acknowledges the validity of Judaism (although she never made a study of Judaism, nor, as far as we know, seriously considered returning to the religious practices and beliefs of her family). After her mother's death, Edith said that she fully expected to see her in heaven, and she made no known overt efforts to evangelize her nieces and nephews, although she welcomed her sister's decision to convert.[10] Therefore, Oben insists that Stein is not a critic of Judaism but a Christian recognizing the validity of the Jewish covenant. (Nonetheless, one is led to point out that Stein did convert rather than investigating and re-committing to the Jewish faith.)[11]

Two statements made by Stein, however, are deeply controversial. In her last will and testament, quoted above, she offers herself 'for the unbelief of the Jewish people' and, as she and Rosa left the monastery in Echt, she is rumored to have said, 'Come, Rosa, we are going for our people.' Both statements can be read as implying the illegitimacy of the 'Old Covenant' and a call for the conversion of all Jews. Eszer himself provides such an interpretation in a letter to a Jewish biographer of Stein, James Baaden (a letter subsequently published in the London *Tablet* and arousing significant alarm). Although Church officials criticized Eszer for his handling of the conversation with Baaden, his comments made explicit what the Jewish community had feared and put in doubt the Church's motives in Stein's beatification and canonization. Would it be used as an opportunity to preach the conversion of all Jews? The Pope avoided all language carrying such implications in both his beatification and canonization messages, but any use of Stein as a bridge between Catholics and Jews does lead one to ask what kind of bridge we are talking about.

Oben, however, disagrees with Eszer, giving a very different reading of Stein's words. She claims that Stein was not in either statement referring to the Jewish religion *per se*. In offering herself for the 'unbelief of the Jews,' Oben argues, Stein was criticizing the atheism present in so many assimilated Jews and certainly characteristic of Stein herself in early years. She is not, therefore, criticizing Jewish beliefs so much as Jewish non-belief. And thus Oben reads Stein as very much in the spirit of *Nostra Aetate* (Declaration on the Relationship of the Church to Non-Christian Religions) and the papal description of Judaism as Christianity's elder brother.[12] Soon after the announcement of Stein's beatification, the Bishops' Committee for Ecumenical and Interreligious Affairs put out a statement, which very much agrees with Oben's interpretation. The Committee insisted on 'the ongoing validity of God's irrevocable covenant with the Jewish people' which is 'solidly founded on our faith in the unshakable faithfulness of God's own word.'[13]

Despite, however, the attempts to show that the beatification and canonization of Stein are not symbolic of a co-opting of the Shoah nor a denigration of Judaism, there are, nonetheless, points of inevitable conflict and real disagreement. Rabbi David Novak puts it well when, in discussing Stein, he insists that for all the reconcili-ation and agreement possible – and as much as it is truly desirable – there are fundamental differences between the Jewish and Christian faiths. And those differences are tied to why some have chosen to become or to remain Jewish and others, Christian. The two religions have different theologies, and these are related to their differing interpretations of history. For Christianity, the central message is Christ. There is a focus on salvation from sin, and Christianity insists that full redemption is possible. To honor a victim of an unspeakable horror, to point to her virtue and to the redemptive – and possibly even expiatory – character of her suffering, to place a monastery at the site of the Shoah (as impolitic as it may be), and to visit with a sorrowful soul, are all actions that reaffirm the Christian message of salvation. Each is the result – perhaps more and less wisely chosen – of an interpretation of the events of history as seen through the salvific story of Christ's birth, death, and resurrection.

The Jewish story, in contrast, is not one of the Incarnation but of the Covenant, and the events of history are seen in the light of God's promise to his people. Likewise, Judaism would reject Stein's claim that suffering can ever be expiatory. One's suffering is only one's own, and one's deeds are only her own. To suffer *for* her people – whether for their Judaism or for their atheism – is an impossibility for a Jew. One may only suffer *with* her people.[14] Fidelity to the Christian faith requires one to be sympathetic and wise, considerate and loving, but it also requires that one hold to the redemptive message of the Cross and its role as the interpretive principle of our lives. And fidelity to Judaism requires a Jewish understanding of the events and a faithful insistence that neither Stein nor the Church can offer forgiveness in the name of the dead. As the two religions differ, so also will their interpretations and perspectives on the events differ.

Stein herself clearly loved her family and cherished her Jewish heritage. A story is told of a conversation she had in Paris in the

1930s during a conference on Thomism and phenomenology. Stein and a friend, also of Jewish descent, were overhead talking affectionately of fellow intellectuals and listing those who were 'one of *ours*,' that is, were Jewish. And she clearly insisted, even as she entered a Carmelite monastery, that it was not her aim to be spared the sufferings of the Jewish people – as, indeed, she was not. But in the end, however, her fundamental commitments were Christian. In a letter to her Prioress, of December 1941, she writes: '[a] *scientia crucis* [knowledge of the Cross] can be gained only when one comes to feel the Cross radically. I have been convinced of that from the first moment and have said, from my heart: *Ave, Crux, spes unica!* [Hail, Cross, our only hope!]' (*Letters*, no. 330), and her final work ends with the words: '[t]hus the bridal union of the soul with God is the end for which the soul was created, bought by the Cross, accomplished on the Cross, and sealed with the Cross for all eternity' (*SC*, p. 207).

Notes

1   There are further related questions regarding who can be considered a Jew and who determines whether one is a Jew. It is clear that Stein understood herself as a Jew, but would or should the Jewish community – then and now, religiously and politically – do so?

2   See Eszer's 'Edith Stein, Jewish Catholic Martyr', pp. 310–27. In 1985 the Pope beatified another victim of the Holocaust, Titus Brandsma, declaring him a martyr who, as a Christian and journalist, publicly protested against Nazi policies. Brandsma was the first Nazi-era martyr, and his beatification may have suggested that a similar course be pursued in Stein's case. One could also look at the case of Maximilian Kolbe, who was canonized in 1982 as a martyr. In all three of these cases, the notion of 'martyr' is broadened somewhat in order, as Eszer argues, to reflect more accurately the contemporary methods of religious persecution.

3   Quoted in Waltraud Herbstrith's *Edith Stein: A Biography*, trans. Bernard Bonowitz (San Francisco, CA: Ignatius Press, 1992), pp. 168–9.

4   The monastery was not built as planned, but placed further away from the camp.

5   Waldheim denied any knowledge of the criminal events in Yugoslavia.

6   Kenneth Woodward, *Making Saints* (see Chapter 1, n. 2), p. 139.

7   In 'A Painful Legacy: Jews and Catholics Struggle to Understand Edith Stein and Auschwitz' in Harry J. Cargas (ed.), *The Unnecessary Problem of Edith Stein* (Lanham, MD: University Press of America, 1994), p. 15.

8 From John Sullivan (ed.), *Holiness Befits Your House: Documentation on the Canonization of Edith Stein* (Washington, DC: ICS Publications, 2000), p. 9.

9 Ecumenical usually refers to discussions *within* one religion and among denominations of, for example, Christianity. In this context, I am following Oben's broader use of the word to include interfaith dialogue.

10 See Batzdorff's *Aunt Edith*, esp. pp. 128 and 161.

11 Several articles have appeared about this issue. See especially Nancy Fuchs-Kreimer's 'Sister Edith Stein: A Rabbi Reacts' in *Lilith*, 16.1 (Winter 1991): 6–7, 28.

12 See *The Life and Thought of St Edith Stein* (New York: Alba House, 2001), esp. Chapter 7.

13 Quoted in Eugene Fisher's article 'A Response to Daniel Polish' in Harry J. Cargas (ed.), *The Unnecessary Problem of Edith Stein*, p. 18.

14 See Susanne Batzdorff's 'Edith Stein aus der Sicht der Verwandten,' Afterword to Matthias Böchel's *Edith Stein und das Judentum*, 2nd edn (Ramstein: Paqué, 1991), pp. 130–9.

Select Bibliography

Works

The publication of the *Edith Steins Werke* [*ESW*] (Edith Stein's Works) began in 1950, ending in 1998. The publication of the critical editions of Stein's work, *Edith Steins Gesamtausgabe* [*ESGA*] (The Collected Editions of Edith Stein), began in 2000 and will continue until all 24 volumes are complete.

Edith Steins Werke [ESW]

I *Kreuzeswissenschaft: Studie über Joannes a Cruce* (Druten: Uitgeverij 'De Maas & Waler', 1950, 1983; Freiburg: Herder, 1950, 1983), trans. Hilda Graef as *The Science of the Cross: A Study of St John of the Cross*. [*SC*] (Chicago: Regnery, 1960; London: Burns & Oates, 1960).

II *Endliches und ewiges Sein: Versuch eines Aufstieges zum Sinn des Seins* [*EeS*: *Finite and Eternal Being*] (Louvain: E. Nauwelaerts, 1950; Freiburg: Herder, 1950, 1962, 1986).

III *Des hl. Thomas von Aquino Untersuchungen über die Wahrheit. Band I* (Louvain: E. Nauwelaerts, 1952). This is a reprint of Stein's translation of Aquinas's *De veritate* (Breslau: O. Borgmeyer, 1932, 1934).

IV *Des hl. Thomas von Aquino Untersuchungen über die Wahrheit. Band II* (Louvain: E. Nauwelaerts, 1955; Freiburg: Herder, 1955).

V *Die Frau: ihre Aufgabe nach Natur und Gnade* (Louvain: E. Nauwelaerts, 1959; Freiburg: Herder, 1959). This is a collection of lectures Stein gave, most of which were published in journals during the 1930s. (Trans. as *CWES* 2.)

VI *Welt und Person: Beitrag zum christlichen Wahrheitsstreben* (Louvain: E. Nauwelaerts, 1962; Freiburg: Herder, 1962).

VII *Aus dem Leben einer jüdischen Familie. Das Leben Edith Steins: Kindheit und Jugend* (Louvain: E. Nauwelaerts, 1965; Freiburg: Herder, 1965). Repr. as *Aus meinem Leben. Mit einer Weiterführung über die zweite Lebenshälfte von Maria Amata Neyer OCD* (Uitgeverij 'De Maas & Waler', 1985; Freiburg: Herder, 1985). (Trans. as *CWES* 1).

VIII *Selbstbildnis in Briefen. Erster Teil: 1916–1934* (Druten: Uitgeverij 'De Maas & Waler', 1976; Freiburg: Herder, 1976). (Trans. with *ESW* IX as *CWES* 5.)

IX *Selbstbildnis in Briefen. Zweiter Teil: 1934–1942* (Druten: Uitgeverij 'De Maas & Waler', 1977; Freiburg: Herder, 1977).

X *Heil im Unheil das Leben Edith Steins. Reife und Vollendung* (Freiburg: Herder, 1983). This is a biography by Romaeus Leuven.

XI *Verborgenes Leben: hagiographische Essays, Meditationen, geistliche Texte* (Druten: Uitgeverij 'De Maas & Waler', 1987; Freiburg: Herder, 1987). (Trans. as *CWES* 4.)

XII *Ganzheitliches Leben: Schriften zur religiösen Bildung* (Freiburg: Herder, 1990).

XIII *Einführung in die Philosophie* (Freiburg: Herder, 1991).

XIV *Briefe an Roman Ingarden: 1917–1938* (Freiburg: Herder, 1991).

XV *Erkenntnis und Glaube* (Freiburg: Herder, 1993). (Trans. as *CWES* 8.)

XVI *Der Aufbau der menschlichen Person* (Freiburg: Herder, 1994).

XVII *Was ist der Mensch?: eine theologische Anthropologie* (Freiburg: Herder, 1994).

XVIII *Potenz und Akt: Studien zu einer Philosophie des Seins* [*Potency and Act*] (Freiburg: Herder, 1998).

Edith Stein Gesamtausgabe [ESGA]

1 *Aus dem Leben einer jüdischen Familie und weitere autobiographische Schriften* (Freiburg: Herder, 2002).

2 *Selbstbildnis in Briefen I (1916–1933)* (Freiburg: Herder, 2000).

3 *Selbstbildnis in Briefen II (1933–1942)* (Freiburg: Herder, 2000).

4 *Selbstbildnis in Briefen III: Briefe an Roman Ingarden* (Freiburg: Herder, 2001).

13 *Die Frau: Fragestellungen und Reflexionen* (Freiburg: Herder, 2000).

16 *Bildung und Entfaltung der Individualität: Beiträge zum christlichen Erziehungsauftrag* (Freiburg: Herder Verlag, 2001).

22 *Übersetzungen II: J.H. Newman, Briefe und Texte zur ersten Lebenshälfte (1801–1846)* (Freiburg: Herder, 2002). This is a reprint of Stein's translation of Newman's letters and papers. (Munich: Theatinerverlag, 1928).

Collected Works of Edith Stein [CWES] (Washington, DC: Institute for Carmelite Studies)

1 *Life in a Jewish Family [Life]*, trans. Josephine Koeppel (1986).

2 *Essays on Woman [EW]*, trans. Freda Mary Oben (1987, rev. edn 1996). Freda Mary Oben has translated additional essays in 'An Annotated Edition of Edith Stein's Papers on Woman' (PhD dissertation, Catholic University of America, Washington, DC, 1979.

3 *On the Problem of Empathy [PE]*, trans. Waltraut Stein (E. Stein's niece), 3rd rev. edn (1989).

4 *The Hidden Life: Hagiographic Essays, Meditations, Spiritual Texts [HL]*, trans. Waltraut Stein (1992).

5 *Self-Portrait in Letters (1916–1942) [Letters]*, trans. Josephine Koeppel (1993).

7 *Philosophy of Psychology and the Humanities [PPH]*, trans. Mary Catharine Baseheart and Marianne Sawicki (2000).

8 *Knowledge and Faith [KF]*, trans. Walter Redmond (2000). The essay 'Husserl's Phenomenology and the Philosophy of St Thomas Aquinas' also appears as an abridged translation in M.C. Baseheart's *Person in the World* (Boston, MA and Dordrecht: Kluwer, 1997), pp. 129–44 and 179–80, and the essay 'Ways to Know God: The "Symbolic Theology" of Dionysius the Areopagite and its Objective Presuppositions' [WG], (trans. M. Rudolf Allers), was originally published in *The Thomist*, 9.3 (July 1946): 379–420.

Forthcoming in CWES:

Finite and Eternal Being, trans. Kurt Reinhardt (expected 2002).
The Science of the Cross, trans. Josephine Koeppel (expected 2002).
An Investigation of the State, trans. Marianne Sawicki.

Other writings

'Die deutsche Summa' in *Die christliche Frau*, 32 (August–September 1934): 245–52; (October 1934): 276–81.

Edith Stein: Essential Writings, ed. John Sullivan (New York: Orbis, 2002).

Edith Stein: Selected Writings, ed. and trans. Susanne M. Batzdorff (Springfield, IL: Templegate Publishers, 1990).

Foreword and commentary in *Adolf Reinach: Gesammelte Schriften* (Halle: Niemeyer, 1921), p. 406 and passim.

'Husserls Exzerpt aus der Staatsexamensarbeit von Edith Stein' (ed. Karl Schuhmann) in *Tijdschrift voor Filosofie*, 53 (1991): 686–99.

'Individuum und Gemeinschaft' (*Beiträge zur philosophischen Begründung der Psychologie und der Geisteswissenschaften, Zweite Abhandlung*) in *Jahrbuch für Philosophie und phänomenologische Forschung*, 5 (1922): 116–283. Trans. in *CWES* 7.

'Der Intellekt und die Intellektuellen' in *Das heilige Feuer*, 18 (1931): 193–8 and 269–72. Repr. in Edith Stein, *Wege zur inneren Stille*, ed. Waltraud Herbstrith (Aschaffenburg: Kaffke, 1987), pp. 98–117.

'Karl Adam's Christusbuch' in *Die Christliche Frau* (March 1933): 84–9.

'La Phénoménologie' in *Journées d'Études de la Société Thomiste* (Juvisy, 12 septembre 1932): 101–11.

'Psychische Kausalität' (*Beiträge zur philosophischen Begründung der Psychologie und der Geisteswissenschaften, Erste Abhandlung*) in *Jahrbuch für Philosophie und phänomenologische Forschung*, 5 (1922): 1–116. Trans. in *CWES* 7.

Review of *Die Abstraktionslehre des hl. Thomas von Aquin*, by L.M. Habermehl, in *Philosophisches Jahrbuch der Görres-Gesellschaft*, 46 (1933): 502–3.

Review of *La Crise de la science et de la philosophie transcendentale. Introduction à la philosophie phénoménologique*, by Edmund Husserl, in *Revue Thomiste* (May–June 1937): 327–9.

Review of *Metaphysik der Gemeinschaft*, by Dietrich von Hildebrand, in *Mädchenbildung auf christlicher Grundlage*, 24 (1932): 695.

Review of *Naturerlebnis und Wirklichkeitsbewusstsein*, by Gertrud Kutznizky, in *Kant-Studien*, 24.4 (1920): 402–5.

'Eine Untersuchung über den Staat' [UüS] in *Jahrbuch für Philosophie und phänomenologische Forschung*, 7 (1925): 1–123, repr. Halle: Niemeyer, 1970.

'Was ist Phänomenologie?' in *Wissenschaft/Volksbindung* – *Wissenschaftliche Beilage zur Neuen Pfälzischen–Zeitung*, 5 (May 15, 1924), repr in *Theologie und Philosophie*, 66 (1991): 570–3.

'Zu Heinrich Gustav Steinmanns Aufsatz, "Zur systematischen Stellung der Phänomenologie"' in Thomas Nenon and Hans Rainer Sepp (eds), *Aufsätze und Vorträge (1911–1921)* (Husserliana 25) (The Hague: Martinus Nijhoff, 1987), pp. 253–66.

Zum Problem der Einfühlung (Halle: Buchdrucheri des Waisenhauses, 1917), repr. München: Kaffke, 1980. (Trans. as *CWES* 3).

'Zur Kritik an Theodor Elsenhans und August Messer' in Thomas Nenon and Hans Rainer Sepp (eds), *Aufsätze und Vorträge (1911–1921)* (Husserliana 25) (The Hague: Martinus Nijhoff, 1987), pp. 226–48.

Further Reading

A relatively comprehensive bibliography of secondary sources is available on the Baltimore Carmel website at *www.geocities.com/baltimorecarmel/stein/borden.html*.

Baseheart, Mary Catharine 'The Encounter of Husserl's Phenomenology and the Philosophy of St Thomas in Selected Writings of Edith Stein' (PhD dissertation, University of Notre Dame, IN, 1960).

—— *Person in the World: Introduction to the Philosophy of Edith Stein* (Boston, MA, and Dordrecht: Kluwer, 1997).

Batzdorff, Susanne M. (E. Stein's niece) *Aunt Edith: The Jewish Heritage of a Catholic Saint* (Springfield, IL: Templegate, 1998).

Bejás, Andrés *Edith Stein: Von der Phänomenologie zur Mystik. Eine Biographie der Gnade* (Disputationes Theologicae 17) (Frankfurt/New York: Peter Lang, 1987).

Brenner, Rachel Feldhay *Writing as Resistance: Four Women Confronting the Holocaust: Edith Stein, Simone Weil, Anne Frank, Etty Hillesum* (Philadelphia, PA: Pennsylvania State University Press, 1997).

Bordeaux, Henry *Edith Stein: Thoughts on her Life and Times*, trans. Donald and Idella Gallagher (Milwaukee, WI: Bruce, 1959).

Cargas, Harry James (ed.) *The Unnecessary Problem of Edith Stein* (*Studies in the Shoah* IV) (Lanham, MD: University Press of America, 1994).

Collins, James 'Edith Stein and the Advance of Phenomenology' in *Thought*, 17 (December 1942): 685–708.

—— 'Edith Stein as a Phenomenologist' in *Three Paths in Philosophy* (Chicago, IL: Henry Regnery, 1962 and 1982), pp. 85–105. Repr. and expanded in 1969 as *Crossroads in Philosophy*.

Eszer, Ambrose 'Edith Stein, Jewish Catholic Martyr' in John Sullivan (ed.), *Edith Stein Symposium: Teresian Culture* (Carmelite Studies 4) (Washington, DC: ICS Publications, 1987), pp. 310–27.

Fetz, Reto Luzius, Rath, Matthias, and Schulz, Peter (eds) *Studien zur Philosophie von Edith Stein* (Internationales Edith-Stein-Symposium Eichstätt 1991/Phänomenologische Forschungen, Bd. 26/27) (München: Alber, 1993).

Gaboriau, Florent *The Conversion of Edith Stein*, trans. Ralph McInerny (South Bend, IN: St Augustine's Press, 2002).

Gerl-Falkovitz, Hanna-Barbara *Unerbittliches Licht. Edith Stein – Philosophie, Mystik, Leben* (Mainz: Matthias-Grünewald, 1991).

Graef, Hilda *The Scholar and the Cross: The Life and Works of Edith Stein* (Westminster, MD: Newman Press, 1955; London and New Work: Longmans, Green, 1955).

—— (ed.) *Writings of Edith Stein* (Westminster, MD: Newman Press, 1956).

Herbstrith, Waltraud *Edith Stein: A Biography*, trans. Bernard Bonowitz (New York: Harper & Row, 1985; San Francisco: Ignatius Press, 1992).

—— (ed.) *Never Forget: Christian and Jewish Perspectives on Edith Stein*, trans. Susanne Batzdorff (Washington, DC: ICS Publications, 1998).

Koeppel, Josephine *Edith Stein: Philosopher and Mystic* (The Way of the Christian Mystics 12) (Collegeville, MN: The Liturgical Press, 1990).

Neyer, Maria Amata *Edith Stein: Her Life in Photos and Documents*, trans. Waltraut Stein (Washington, DC: ICS Publications, 1999).

Oben, Freda Mary *Edith Stein: Scholar, Feminist, Saint* (Staten Island, NY: Alba House, 1988).

—— *Life and Thought of St Edith Stein* (New York: Alba House, 2001).

Posselt, Teresa (Sr Teresia de Spiritu Sancto, Stein's novice mistress and later prioress in Cologne) *Edith Stein*, trans. Cecil Hastings and Donald Nicholl (London, New York: Sheed & Ward, 1952).

Reifenrath, Bruno H. *Erziehung im Lichte des Ewigen: Die Pädagogik Edith Steins* (Berlin, Frankfurt, Munich: Moritz Diesterweg, 1985).

Sawicki, Marianne *Body, Text and Science: The Literacy of Investigative Practices and the Phenomenology of Edith Stein* (Boston, MA, and Dordrecht: Kluwer, 1997).

Secretan, Philibert *Erkenntnis und Aufstieg: Einführung in die Philosophie von Edith Stein* (Innsbruck: Tyrolie-Verlag, 1992).

Sullivan, John (ed.) *Holiness Befits Your House: Documentation on the Canonization of Edith Stein* (Washington, DC: ICS Publications, 2000).

Van den Berg, M. Regina 'Community in the Thought of Edith Stein' (PhD dissertation, Catholic University of America, Washington, DC, 2000).

Index

Page references in **bold** indicate the main discussion of the entry.

151